'This is a highly readable, accessible and stimulating instant ease of understanding the creative mind and the creative process and in finding ways to rally one's working colleagues. Read it from cover to cover first up... or dip in and out as fancy takes you. You won't be disappointed. Creativity rules... and long may she reign.'

— Kay Kimber, Griffith University, Director, Centre for Continuing Professional Learning Faculty of Education

---

'I've been a creative my whole life and watched as corporations have little or no understanding of how valuable and viable we are. I've seen so many other creatives get shot down only to withhold their ideas in the future.

This book breaks open new boundaries. There is nothing out there like it that I have ever seen. This book is of great value to all corporations because creativity comes forth at all levels.'

— Leo Procopio, MBA, Creative Director STLEO LLC

'Nigel has once again produced a book that is practical and easy to read with excellent tips to lead creativity in your team and organisation. Creativity is now regarded as the key leadership attribute of our time. May this book help inspire everyone to unlock their unique creative contributions and achieve extraordinary results in the process'.

— Tania de Jong AM, Founder Creativity Australia and CEO Creative Universe

Disclaimer
All the information, techniques, skills and concepts contained
within this publication are of the nature of general comment
only, and are not in any way recommended as individual advice.
The intent is to offer a variety of information to provide a wider
range of choices now and in the future, recognising that we all
have widely diverse circumstances and viewpoints. Should any
reader choose to make use of the information contained herein,
this is their decision, and the author and publisher does not
assume any responsibilities whatsoever under any conditions
or circumstances. It is recommended that the reader obtain their
own independent advice.

FIRST EDITION 2010
Copyright © 2010 Through Design Pty Ltd

1st ed.
ISBN 978-0-9775735-1-6

(Series: Leading Creatives).

Published by Nigel Collin Creative
A division of Through Design Pty Ltd
PO Box 712, North Ryde, NSW 1670 Australia
Email: support@nigelcollin.com
Website: www.nigelcollin.com

For further information about orders:
Phone: +61 2 98886200
Email: support@nigelcollin.com

Editing by Megan Kerr [www.megankerr.co.uk]
Design by 2birds design [www.2birds.com.au]

Herding Monkeys

How to Lead the Creative Talents of Your People
and Turn Their Ideas into Commercial Results

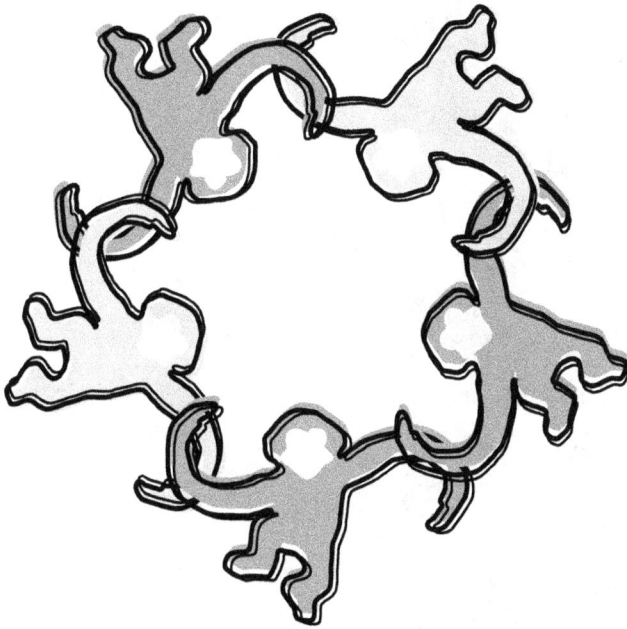

Nigel Collin

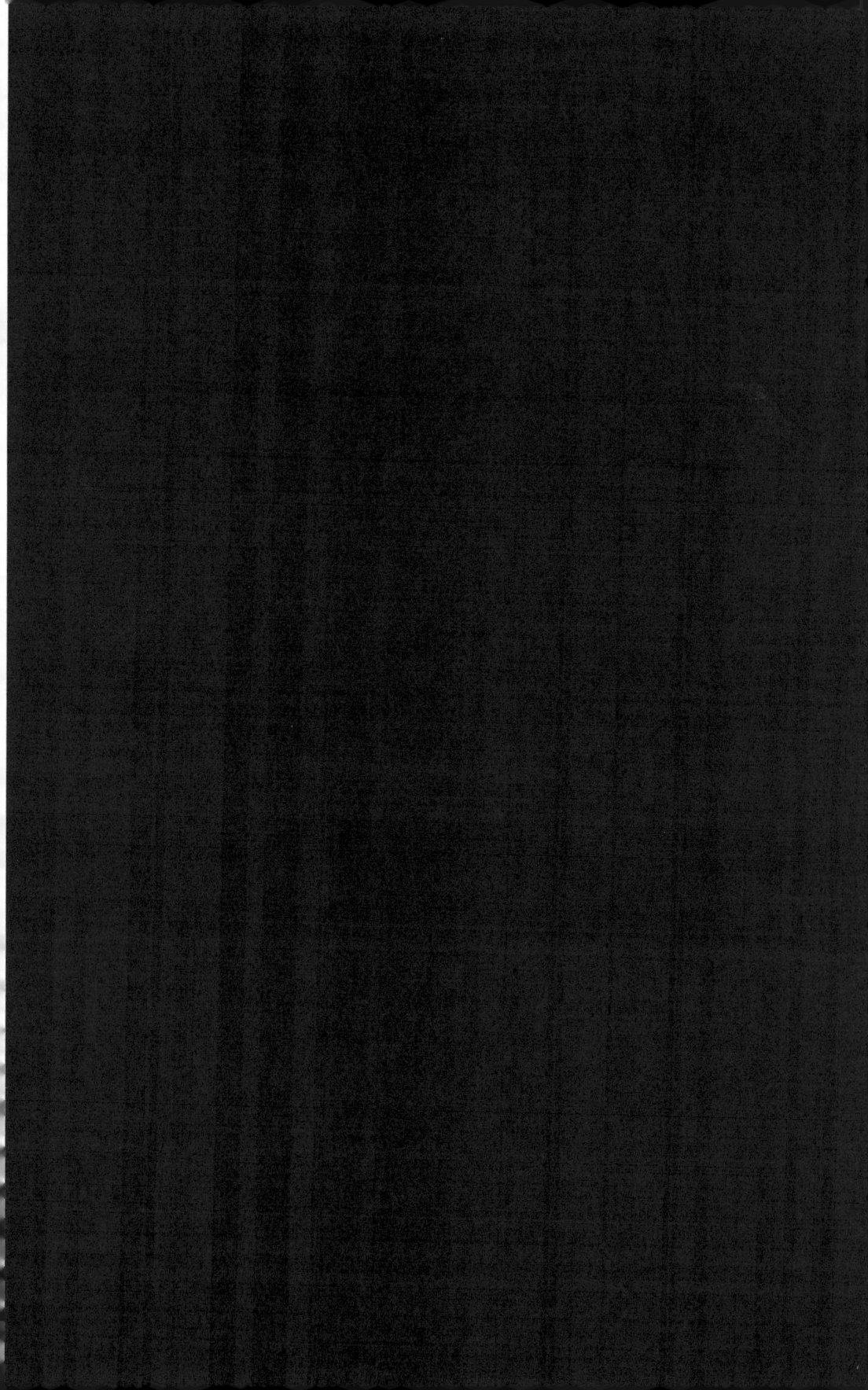

Start Here:

WHAT'S THIS BOOK ALL ABOUT THEN?

This book is about how to get the most from your creative people and creative teams. It's not about being more creative or generating ideas — it's about inspiring and nurturing the creativity of others. It's about leading the creativity in your business, so you get the commercial results you need and achieve real business value.

After 15 years working in the creative sector, with creative people and teams, I've come to understand this: the challenge that businesses face with creativity isn't finding creative people or teaching them to be more creative. The challenge is leading your creative people and drawing on their talents. How do you tap into and harness their genius, then direct it towards viable business outcomes?

Leading creative people is like herding monkeys. They seem to be all over the place, off in a world of their own. But they're also very communal and enjoy hanging out with other creative types. They're brilliant at slinging stuff; they're always throwing ideas, designs, and concepts around. They are incredibly smart. And you need them, as much as they need you.

MONKEYS, ZOOS, AND DUCKS

To capitalise on the creative talents of your people and your business, a great leader must focus on three things: Herding Monkeys, Creating Zoos, and Shooting Ducks. In other words, you need to focus on leadership, culture, and process. Here's what this series of books will cover:

---

1. HERDING MONKEYS — LEADERSHIP

Leading creative people is like *herding monkeys*. Because they think, feel, and do differently, you need a different set of leadership skills.

---

2. CREATING ZOOS — CULTURE

You also need to build an environment that supports and stimulates creativity, where creative people feel inspired and safe to be creative. So you need to build a *creative zoo*.

---

3. SHOOTING DUCKS — PROCESS

You need a process in place where coming up with ideas is like *shooting ducks* at a carnival. The truth is, there's no shortage of ideas. The trick is focusing on and carrying out the right ones.

This book focuses on *herding monkeys*. It will touch on the other aspects, because they influence each other and they do overlap. Leadership, however, (to steal J.R.R. Tolkien's phrase) is the 'one ring that rules them all'. And *that's* what this book is about. So here's what we'll look at...

LEADERSHIP

CULTURE

PROCESS

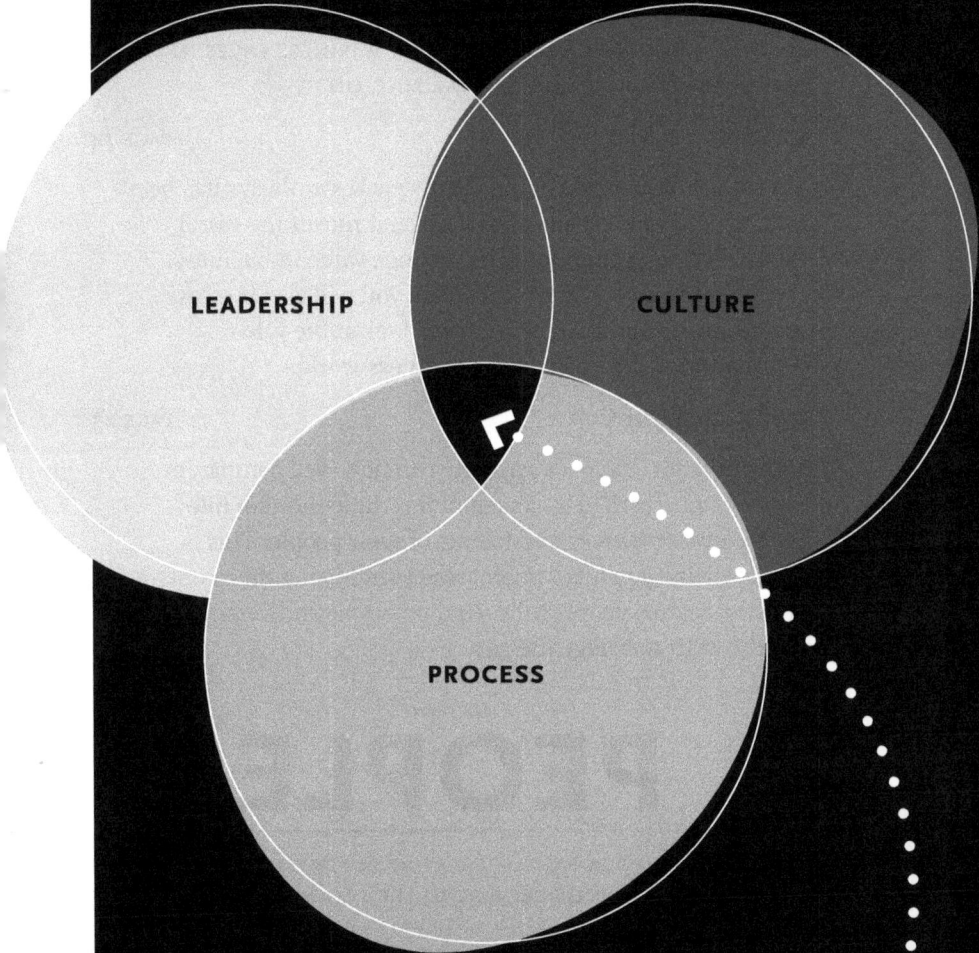

Creative sweet spot

There's no denying it. Being creative is sexy. Always has been. It drives economies, enriches lives, and moves the world forward. More importantly, it has huge value in business. If you increase your creative capital, you will also increase the value of your business. So we'll look at the value proposition of creativity in the business world.

Unfortunately, there's a gap between how well companies understand creativity's value and how little they tap into the creative resources and talents of their people. This is the creativity gap. Most businesses aren't using the talents of their creative people fully. And once you understand why, you can start to bridge the gap.

Some people are more creative than others and we should be thrilled about that. That's why we have creative teams — but that shouldn't exclude others. The truth is that creative people are everywhere, at all levels of your organisation. We need to understand where the creative people are and who they are, so we can tap the gold vein of their talents.

04 Being the right leader

The role of a leader of creative people is crucial and because creatives think, feel, and act very differently, you need a different set of leadership skills. To lead creative people effectively, you need to be a nurturer and custodian of their talents. You need to be a mentor and a coach. You need to know how to inspire them, empower them, guide them, earn their respect, and let them play. The *last* thing you want to be is their boss.

05 What Motivates Creatives?

To lead anyone effectively, you need to know what motivates them, inspires them, and turns them on. Creative people reap great benefits working for an organisation: you need to know what those are so you can give them more of it. You have to know what they need to do their jobs and how you can deliver it. Give them what they need so they can give you what you need.

PART THREE

IN PRACTICE

FINALLY, WE'LL BRING IT ALL TOGETHER AND LOOK AT WHAT YOU NEED TO DO AS A LEADER TO HELP YOUR CREATIVES BE THEIR VERY BEST, SO YOU GET THE VERY BEST OUTCOMES.

06 Casting

Putting creative teams together is an art in itself, much like casting a film. If you get the mix wrong, it can cause all sorts of dramas — but if you get the mix right, it rocks. It takes your creative capital to a whole new level. This isn't just about the 'best' people; it's also about combining the right people. In short, it's getting the best-right mix. We'll look at what you need to consider when putting together a great creative team.

07 Getting Ownership

If you want your people to get fired up about their creativity and their ideas, and follow them through, then you need them to take ownership of those ideas. Not because they have to, but because they want to. When your people take ownership, you can't *stop* them giving you extraordinary results.

08 Creative Risk

Being creative is a risky business, but the Number One killer of creativity in an organisation is risk aversion. Business likes progress and success, not failure, but trying new things means falling over every so often. Many great ideas and achievements have come from making mistakes. Failure holds great value and potential success if you recognise it, capture it, and turn it to your advantage.

09 The Freedom of Structure

One of the great ironies of creativity is that to have the creative freedom you need, you also need a creative structure. Creativity loves structure, it thrives on it, but get it wrong and you'll either restrict it or have it meander about without any direction. So you need to have the right creative process, one that knows when to turn the creative controls on and off.

10 Let's Crack Open the Bubbly and Celebrate

It's important to celebrate creative successes. Celebrating is more than having a good time and it's more than just bonding. It says, 'This chapter has finished,' so that the next one can start cleanly, without shadows or overtones from what went previously. It gives closure and resets the creative switch. It reinforces a sense of community and shows appreciation. It keeps the creative reservoir refilled.

11 The Quest

To be a great leader of creative people and for your business to lead its industry creatively, you need to inspire the creativity in others. Each of us has huge power to influence the creativity of others, whether we recognise it or not. If each of us can inspire just one person to be more creative, and empower just one person to inspire someone else's creativity, then together we will have begun to change not only the creative landscape of a business but the creative landscape of the world. And that is a quest worth taking.

Let's start.

PART

ONE

PREMISE

01: Creative is Sexy

Creative is sexy. It always has been. It's sexy because everybody is talking about it and everybody is doing it. And if you're not, you want to be doing it, and if you are, you want to be doing it better.

But creativity is also sexy because it holds huge value. It drives new ideas and innovations; it drives economies and contributes to society. For individuals, it helps build self-confidence and self-esteem. It gives us a voice and an outlet for our artistic sides.

In business, creativity is even sexier. It holds enormous benefits, allowing businesses to outpace competition, solve problems, find opportunities, and harness change. It adds value to an organisation's people, its customers, and ultimately to its bottom line.

Log onto any business website, such as Business Week or Harvard Business Review, search for 'creativity', and you'll find a plethora of articles. Open any business journal and you're likely to find articles and editorials on creativity and its place in the world.

In June 2010, Fast Company published a special issue listing 'The 100 Most Creative People in Business'. In May 2010, IBM released a report titled 'Capitalizing on Complexity — Insights from the Global Chief Executive Officer Study' which stated that 'CEOs cited creativity as the most important leadership quality over the next five years'.

All this is nothing new. We all innately understand the value creativity holds. It has always been important and has always been there. Never doubt it: creativity is crucial and has moved society, our world, and our lives forward. Without it, life would be bland and go nowhere. Nothing new or exciting happens unless someone, somewhere, has that creative spark light up in their heads.

In a world that is constantly changing, creativity is the ultimate weapon. It doesn't just allow you to cope, but also allows you to take advantage of change. And yes, CEOs of major organisations knows this, but it's not only the domain of big companies. Every business, no matter how big or small, can and should commercialise creativity, because the world will keep on changing.

THE WONDERFUL WORLD OF CHANGE

Working with a client in New Zealand a while back, I came across a billboard in the main street of Auckland, across which was written, 'By the time you finish reading this, the world will have changed.'

I love that. I love it because it's true; who would argue with it? The world is changing. People will also tell you that the world *is* changing faster than it ever has before. But here's the thing. The world has *always* changed and it has also always been changing faster than it ever has before.

'By the time you finish reading this, the world will have changed.'

Think about it. If you lived in the Industrial Revolution, the rate of change compared to any other time in history was alarming. Factories were popping up everywhere, lifestyles were changing, there was social upheaval, motor vehicles, and electricity. It must have been mind-blowing. And if you grew up just before everything started, the world you knew would've changed beyond recognition in front of your very eyes.

Go back even further, to medieval Europe. If you were alive then, you'd have been amazed at how your village was burgeoning, at how many people suddenly appeared at the Saturday market from all over the place. If you were a potato merchant, no doubt you'd have fretted over the stock you had to produce to cope with demand — and how were you ever going to get your potatoes carried across the village to the market in time? Maybe someone would invent a larger barrow. Add to that the political unrest, the plague, landlords, and crusades: life must have been an ever-evolving tapestry.

We shouldn't use clichés but this calls for a golden oldie: 'The only constant is change itself.' Creativity is a major tool for coping with change, because it allows us to adapt, be agile, and find innovative solutions.

More importantly, though, creativity allows us to take advantage of change. We can find opportunities and use change to our benefit. We can get proactive instead of being reactive. It also helps us to instigate change and be ahead of the pack.

CHANGE IS UNPREDICTABLE

Let me take you back to the first century AD, when Rome was at her peak and led the civilised world. If you lived in Roman times, under Roman rule, you'd have lived in an incredibly advanced civilisation. The Romans built roads, aqueducts, and sewage pipes. It wasn't all gladiators, armies, and politics; Rome was an engineering marvel. So much so that you might've thought it wasn't possible to advance any further. How could you? Things were better than they'd ever been! One of Rome's most prominent sons, an engineer named Julius Frontinus, declared, 'Inventions have long since reached their limit and I see no hope for further development.'

Jump forward to more modern times. In 1927, when talking pictures hit Hollywood, H.M. Warner said, 'Who wants to hear actors talk?' In 1949, an article on popular mechanics stated that, 'Computers in the future will weigh no more than five tons,' — mathematically accurate, but hardly prescient. And if we're honest with ourselves, at some point in lives we've all told someone (perhaps even ourselves) those famous last words, 'You can't do that!' — only to be proved wrong.

REFUSING CHANGE

Let's head back to Hollywood in 1927, when the world changed dramatically forever. Hollywood was in its prime, producing more films than any other time in history — up to 800 a year. Stars like Rudolph Valentino and Mary Pickton were considered Gods and no doubt Saturday matinees were every bit as popular as iPhones, Playstations, and Nintendo Wii today.

But in 1927, great change was afoot: the 'Talking Pictures' arrived.

You can't stay in your corner of the Forest waiting for others to come to you. You have to go to them sometimes.

— WINNIE THE POOH (A.A. MILNE)

For many, the advent of sound was a major upheaval and created imponderable challenges. Film studios were forced to build new sound 'stages'; clunky and noisy cameras became useless; directors and technicians had to rethink and reinvent camera movements and microphone placements — and all to accommodate 'talkies' and the new technology they required.

Many actors were unlucky. With heavy accents or shrill voices, some simply didn't manage the transition from silent to sound and their careers ended abruptly. Silent stars such as Agnes Ayers, Emil Jannings, and Gilbert Rowland (nope, I hadn't heard of them either) saw their careers snatched from beneath them.

The advent of sound changed the film industry forever and, with it, the lives and careers of many. Some adapted, got creative, and thrived; others didn't. Take Charlie Chaplin — now there's a name we *have* heard of. Chaplin was a Hollywood God. He entertained millions and influenced countless actors (and still does). He brought vaudeville to Hollywood, cofounded United Artists, and is, without doubt, still considered one the Hollywood greats.

But Chaplin refused to have his 'little tramp' character talk. He said of sound in films, 'Action is more generally understood than words.' He clearly felt that the tramp's speaking would undermine and detract from his endearing, pantomime character. Although he added musical tracks to films such as *City Lights*, he only ever spoke once — briefly, in *The Great Dictator*, to mock Hitler. No-one would dispute the legacy he left behind. Chaplin is synonymous with silent film. And there lies the rub.

The tramp didn't or couldn't make the transition from silent to sound. Chaplin failed to adapt fully to the 'talkies' and create an opportunity from them. He made countless films before the advent of sound, but only a handful afterwards.

EMBRACING CHANGE

In contrast, let's look at someone who saw the dawn of sound not as a hurdle but as an opportunity, and turned it to his advantage. In 1928, only a year after sound arrived, a small mouse made his debut in the world's first talking cartoon, *Steamboat Willie*, and stunned the film world and audiences alike.

With *Steamboat Willie*, Walt Disney had truly arrived. He saw an opportunity in sound and went with it. It wasn't a one-off: Disney had a knack for sensing change, getting creative, and turning it to his advantage.

In the 1950s, another enormous change rocked Hollywood and the world forever: television. Once again, Disney was ready to take advantage. Some said television would destroy the film industry. Why would people go see films when they could watch shows in their own home? But as the cofounder of one of Hollywood's leading studios, Disney didn't see television as a threat. He saw an opportunity to be used to his advantage.

Thinking differently to everyone else, Disney had an idea. At the time, he was creating 'Disneyland' and needed capital to get it up and running. Television, he realised, was a fundraiser and a promotional tool for his new project. He made a deal with a major network, provided an exclusive weekly show, *Disneyland*, and got the funding he needed. What's more, as viewers all over America tuned in to watch, Disney showed them snippets of the park being built, exciting his potential guests.

Talking pictures and the advent of television were two quantum leaps beyond the control of most people in Hollywood. Some crashed and some survived; some saw change as opportunity, got creative, and took control.

Change is always present and it's not going to go away. The question is how we deal with it. Do we hide our heads in the sand? Or do we start to reinvent ourselves, get proactive, see the opportunities that change will bring, and start getting creative?

The creative companies — the ones that not only have great ideas but also make creativity a key organisational value — are best placed to deal with changes in their industry and their market, to adapt to new technologies and trends, and to maintain a competitive edge.

The question is: in the face of change, are you going to be Walt Disney or Charlie Chaplin?

THE NEW CREATIVE ECONOMY

In his book *Flight of the Creative Class*, Richard Florida talks about the role creativity plays in driving economies. He points out that in the US alone, workers in the creative sector make up 30% of the workforce and earn nearly 50% of the money.

In Australia, 'the creative economies now account for approximately 35% of Australian jobs with this figure continuing to increase and our international partners are making significant and bold strides towards mainstreaming creativity,' according to the Queensland Department of Education, Training and the Arts, in their report, 'Year of Creativity 2009'. This was a report on the minister's roundtable for the year of creativity (of which I can proudly say I was a part).

Being creative is not some whimsical, intangible thing, but a real force when it comes to making a buck.

Richard Florida also talks about the indispensable role that society plays in attracting creative people and supporting their talents. He calls them 'the creative class'. The premise is that cities and countries who understand the economic benefits that creativity pays are beginning to attract the right people and tap into this rich resource. He gives a 'creative countries global index', listing which countries are considered to be the most creative of all. Sweden is first, then Japan, then Finland; the US is fifth and Australia twelfth.

If cities and countries recognise the important role that creative people play, then so should we.

If cities and countries recognise the important role that creative people play, then so should we.

CEOs VALUE CREATIVITY

As mentioned above, the IBM 'Capitalizing on Complexity' report reflects the IBM Global CEO Study, where they interviewed over 1500 CEOs from 33 industries. The report points out that 'the degree of difficulty CEOs anticipate, based on the swirl of complexity, has brought them to an inflection point. Asked to prioritize the three most important leadership qualities in the new economic environment, creativity was the one they selected more than any other choice.'

It also states that 'It's not that CEOs are just now becoming aware of the importance of creativity — they have long been aware of the need to innovate their products, their processes and their customers' experiences. Even in 2004, CEOs were telling us that "CEOs the world over were refocused on growth, and they viewed innovation as the way to get there." But today, creativity itself has been elevated to a leadership style.

Traditional approaches to managing organizations need fresh ideas — ideas that are intended to disrupt the status quo.'

What does than mean? First, it confirms creativity's place in the business world. More than that, it places creativity on a pedestal. It also shows that the CEOs of major organisations around the world recognise creativity's vital important in navigating the business world and economic climate. And to a large extent, it reinforces Richard Florida's 'new creative economy'. One comment in the report from a telecommunications CEO in India sums it up very nicely: 'Creativity is everything.'

CREATIVITY DRIVES INNOVATION

In business circles, creativity is often held up as the little brother of innovation. The two are also often lumped together and used in the same sentence. Although they do fit together nicely, they are in fact two very different beasts.

Innovation implements ideas; creativity generates them.

In essence, innovation is the application and implementation of ideas. That's why it's so important to business: innovation leads to strategies and inventions; it gives ideas and concepts a place in the world. Unless an idea is put into play, it doesn't contribute to the overall health or bottom line of the company.

Being creative, on the other hand, is about *generating* concepts, strategies, and ideas. It's the *thinking* part. Without it, innovation would have a tough time because there would be nothing to innovate. I find it interesting that the IBM study listed creativity as Number One quality and not innovation. Innovation can be seen as a result and flow-on of creativity. Creativity feeds the innovation pipeline. They are intrinsically linked, but creativity is at the forefront.

Innovation implements ideas; creativity generates them.

COMMERCIALISING CREATIVITY

The IBM study clearly shows the importance of creativity as a leadership skill. But what about commercialising creativity, getting results, and being a successful creative company?

One of the best examples of how creativity can be commercialised is Disney. They're also the ultimate example of how to inspire and capture the creative talents of individuals, then harness that talent. I'll keep coming back to Disney, not just because I like them, but because there are great lessons to be found there. Of course they're not the only one. Look around and you'll see fantastic examples of creative companies everywhere: Virgin, Google, Ogilvy, 3M... the list goes on and on.

Apple also always makes the 'Great Creative Company Case-study' list. Undeniably, they're one of those companies that just oozes creativity. Not only are they renowned for their design and user-friendliness, but they change our world. The iPhone changed more than how we use a phone — it changed how we interface with virtually everything. The iPod changed more than how we listen to music — it changed how we buy music.

Creative companies abound. By looking at some of them and seeing what they do, we'll discover many practical hints and lessons to draw upon, adopt, and adapt. Oodles of books are written about these creative juggernauts — it's not my intention to add to the list, but from time to time we'll drop in and visit some of them.

APPLE ENVY

But let's face it: most of us aren't Apple.

You don't need to be envious of Apple.

And it's dangerous to focus solely on these creative juggernauts, thinking that only massive companies such as the Apples, Virgins, Googles, and Disneys of the world are can bring massive creative endeavours to life.

That simply isn't true. You'll find creative businesses anywhere and everywhere, from your corner pizza shop to your local design agency to major fashion houses, film studios, and advertising agencies, from small engineering firms to international consulting companies.

Being creative is not the exclusive domain of giants. Even Apple started out as a small entity. Prior to that, it was a creative spark just waiting to be ignited. Disney didn't start out as the largest entertainment and media conglomerate in the world either. It started with Walt and his brother Roy.

Some of the most creative businesses are right under our noses.

Let me take you back to 1902, when an enterprising young man had an idea. J.A. Birchall owned a small stationary shop in Launceston, Tasmania.

Back at the turn of the century, if you wanted to communicate with your clients, you couldn't email or text them. You would jump on your horse and head off across town, or you would write to them. But unlike today's world, you bought writing paper in large individual sheets, usually rolled, that you would then cut to size and use.

Our hero, young Mr Birchall, had an idea. He wrote to his suppliers in England and suggested they cut the sheets down into smaller, more manageable sizes. He then evolved the idea and suggested they place a firm backing board under the sheets so you didn't have to roll them. He took it even further and suggested they get some gum and glue the top edges of the loose sheets together, so people could peel them off, one by one, as they needed them.

It took a while to convince his suppliers, but eventually J.A. Birchall's creative scheme came into existence. An Australian, a Tasmanian from Launceston, invented the writing notepad that we know today.

What's cool is that Birchall's still exists and on their website they boast the creative endeavours they hold as a company.

Sydney-based software firm Atlassian began life in Sydney in 2002. According to their website, Scott Farquhar and Mike Cannon-Brookes started the company with $10,000 charged to their Visa card. Today, Atlassian boasts offices in Sydney, San Francisco, and Amsterdam, with over 270 employees and 24,000 customers in more than 138 countries. They must be doing something right. Incidently these figures keep growing and by the time you read this, they will no doubt be higher still.

One of the keys for Atlassian is its people. When asked how important creative people were to Atlassian, Community Coordinator Robyn Munro replied, 'They are very important, as they keep us ahead of our competition. In an industry as fast-paced as information technology and software development, it is imperative that you are not just copying your competitors — rather, that you are leading the field, be it in design, functionality, or product features.'

Atlassian is a fantastic example of a 'creative company' thriving in the current business and economic world. And they're a relatively small (well, small-ish) company who are doing everything right when it comes to being creative, working with creative people, and getting commercial results. We'll revisit them in the following chapters for tips and ideas.

You don't need to be envious of Apple.

THE NUTSHELL

Creativity plays a vital role in our lives and our world. To finish where we started, Creative is Sexy. It's all good news. And in business, creative is even sexier, because it can add real value to your bottom line.

Innately, though, we all know this.

I could spend the entire book building the case for creativity in the business world, but I'd rather assume that you get it. We all get it. And if any of us don't quite yet, best to study up on the topic or the world will sail on by — there's a reading list at the end of the book.

As with any good-news story, there is also a downside. There are several inherent problems with bringing creativity to life in an organisation. We call this the *creativity gap*.

02: The Creativity Gap

The bad news: creativity doesn't come without pitfalls. The good news: once we understand what the pitfalls are, we can overcome them and move on. Business faces a real problem in regards to creativity. It's called the *creativity gap.*

There's a gap between the value an organisation places on being creative and its ability to tap into its creative resources, the talents of its creative people. You may understand the whole 'creativity has massive value' proposition, but actually making it work for you and delivering that value is a completely different game.

How do I know this? My business conducted a survey of both business leaders and creative people[1] and one of the questions we asked was, 'In business, should creativity have a commercial value?' Pretty straightforward and, as you would expect, most people answered yes — 90%, in fact. Hardly surprising. In the commercial world, creativity simply isn't useful unless it leads to a positive business outcome[*].

Try it yourself: ask a roomful of business people the same question and you'll get a similar response. Most people get the value proposition.

BUT... the surprise came from another fairly straightforward question: 'Do you feel your company utilises the talents of your creative people to the fullest?' Sit for a while and think about how you would respond. You may even know your answer immediately.

[*] The Survey had 182 respondents from variety of creative industries, comprising both business leaders and creative people

Only 17% of people answered yes. That rings alarm bells for me — in fact, it sets off air-raid sirens.

On the one hand, business emphatically understands the need for creativity to be commercially valuable; on the other, 83% don't make full use of their creative people's abilities and wisdom to achieve this. What's even more amazing is that they know they don't!

It's like building a bridge across a canyon to get a heap of stuff to the other side, but only using 17% of that bridge's capacity. You have to limit how much you carry across and do multiple trips. It's inefficient: you're not making full use of a perfectly useful bridge. You wouldn't use only 17% of the bridge's capacity, so why only 17% of your organisation's creative capacity?

Why is this? Why is there this gap? The answer to comes down to two things — perception and understanding what makes creativity tick.

THE INTANGIBLE BEAST

Business tend to have three key perceptions about creativity and creative people. And these perceptions, or rather misperceptions, determine how business deals with creativity and goes against the creative grain.

Let me introduce you to the intangible beast.

Most people and most organisations see creativity as a whaffly, whimsical beast. A mythical, imponderable being, extremely hard to define and pin down. A kind of 'out there' type of thing, untamed, unstructured, and difficult to harness. As a result, it's greatly misunderstood and mishandled.

In our quest to understand the beast and make sense of it, three things happen and none of them productive. The ramifications of trying to understand and control the intangible nature of the beast are, in fact, destroying the value creativity holds for our businesses.

We all know the beast exists, but we all have different perceptions of it — different perspectives on what it looks like, how it behaves, and what it does. To give the beast some shape and form, the first thing we do is try to define it.

We hunt far and wide for a definition of what creativity really *is* and what exactly it looks like. And that is very, very difficult.

Ask a roomful of people what creativity is and you will get a roomful of different answers.

One of the exercises we do in our workshops is to get everyone to bring along a symbol of what creativity means to them. What you get is never the same. For one person, the symbol is a blank sheet of paper, because it has infinite possibilities. For another, it's a child's painting, because it represents an ability to explore and seek possibilities. For someone else, it's a bust of Charles Darwin, because it represents the ever-evolving nature of ideas. And on it goes.

The very act of defining creativity destroys the essence of what it is.

Being creative means different things to different people and we all see creativity in different ways. At school, we were each encouraged or discouraged to be creative and that in turn influences or taints our view of the creative world. Perhaps, early on, we were told how important creativity is in the world, that it's a noble pursuit — or maybe someone told us to get a 'real job', something that pays the bills. That also shapes our view of creativity's place in the world.

Our perception of creativity is a personal one. But take the personal factor out, and you are still left with a kaleidoscope of definitions as to what creativity is, what role it plays, and the value it holds.

To find a definition, you could do a Google search, look it up in a dictionary, or ask a scholar, and you will end up with many different answers. They vary from 'the creation of something new' to 'the convergence of old and existing ideas to create something unique' to 'out of the box' to 'a cerebral process', and infinitely on. Add the context to that — are you an artist, a business leader, a graphic designer, a university student? — or why you're defining it, and you get a whole new layer.

Facilitating a breakfast on 'Finding the value of creativity', I once asked 'What's the definition of creativity?' Then I sat back and let the room go for it. If you ever need to fill half a day in a creative workshop, just ask that.

The truth is that creativity is very difficult to define. And there lies a trap: the very act of defining creativity destroys the essence of what it is.

Being creative is all about finding new possibilities, going where no mind has ever gone before, seeing the world from completely different points of view, thinking differently, and finding new perspectives. Once we define it, there is no room for any of that, because the definition limits it. If you say, 'Creativity is *this*,' then you cannot say, 'Creativity is *that*.' It goes against the nature of the beast.

Creativity is all about exploring and discovering. If you drew a map of creativity, depicted the lay of the land, meticulously studied and recorded every detail, marked out all the terrain and its contours, built a legend with finite scales of measurement, and positioned a border around the outside, then there would be no more exploration because there'd be nothing left to explore. There'd be no more discovering, because there'd be nothing left to discover. Creating a map means you know the terrain. Creativity needs to leave the sanctity of the map and go beyond into uncharted waters.

The process of trying to define creativity goes against everything it stands for and in turn actually destroys it.

2. WE TRY TO DEFINE THEM

The second thing we do is we try to define who is and who isn't creative. We often see creative people as this select few, who have dreadlocks or ponytails, who spend years at fashion or film school, who ride pushbikes to the office and spend most of their day drinking coffee. That's already dangerous, because it creates a great divide, an us-and-them scenario.

By labelling certain people as 'creative', we're in fact excluding everybody else. That narrows potential creative input. Creativity is all about finding new possibilities — and so, ironically, if we limit our view of 'creative people', we in fact limit our possibilities and we're ultimately not being very creative.

So Part II of this book is all about people: who creative people are and what motivates them, but also who you are as their leader.

3. WE TRY TO DEFINE HOW TO DO IT

The final thing we do in our quest to understand and tame the beast is probably the most dangerous of all. We try to systemise the creative process to the nth degree.

Let's face it, business likes tangible. And creativity is anything but tangible. Business likes certainty: it likes things to be black and white. Creativity is anything but black and white — it isn't even grey, it's multicoloured. It's full of paradox, contradiction, and ambiguity.

In a vain attempt to make the beast tangible and give it certainty, businesses grab hold of the beast, wrestle with it, and once they get a decent grip on it, they shove it into a cage and lock it up. Once that's done, they can turn to their colleagues and clients and say, 'Look! There it is! And not only do we have Creativity, but we also have control over it.'

In the quest to make creativity tangible and concrete, to justify and quantify it, once again we only end up destroying it.

So Part III looks at how to manage creativity within business and within projects, and how to find that balance between freedom and structure.

It's important to focus on how to nurture, support, and lead your creative people.

DON'T CHANGE THE BEAST

If the goal is to draw on the creative nature of the beast, what's the solution? How do you deal with it?

Try this, instead. What if you *don't* try to define the beast, but simply learn to accept it for what is? What if you try to *understand* the beast and help the beast understand you? What if you come to terms with its ambiguous nature? After all, the beast is what the beast is. Creativity is what creativity is.

What if, rather than locking it up in a cage and trying to control its every move, you simply let the beast roam around, doing what it needs to do and being what it needs to be? It will be happy and content.

Once you understand creativity and accept it for what it is, you can begin to work with it rather than against it. So let's try understanding it. What makes the beast tick?

A BRIEF GUIDE TO INTANGIBLE-BEAST KEEPING

It's important to focus on how to nurture, support, and lead your creative people. To do that, you provide the best possible resources, build the best teams and communities, find out what turns them on, and do everything you can to ensure you are supporting and applying their creative talents to the fullest. Once you get to know your creative people and gain their confidence and respect, extraordinary things happen.

But you also need to recognise what you do that gets in the way. What impedes creativity and prevents your people from being as creative as they can be? Sometimes we spend so much time focusing on what to do that we forget to focus on what not to do.

So it's worth taking time to look at what really annoys and frustrates creative people, and also the things business does to stifle and kill creativity in its tracks. Because, unfortunately, business is often good at doing just that — and as a result it just ends up irritating its creative people and ultimately fails to tap into their true genius.

You also need to know what turns creative people on, what motivates and drives them. Because when you help creative people to be their very best, then the creativity within your business will soar.

So here are the key basics: what drives the beast crazy, what kills it, and what feeds it? We'll come back to these later with some strategies for each one.

We have to continually be jumping off cliffs and developing our wings on the way down.

—KURT VONNEGUT

Here's a list of ten ways to absolutely frustrate creative people and in the process kill off their creativity and passion. Guaranteed!

1. tell them how

2. don't respect them

3. give them loads of red tape

4. don't tolerate their mistakes

5. segregate them

6. same, same, same

7. contain their expertise

8. play the money game

9. act superior

10. have lots of long meetings

This list is like a red rag to the intangible beast. If you're brave enough to ask yourself if you recognise any of them, the chances are you do. But that's okay, because here's the positive spin: once you know what they are and you're aware of them, you can start to deal with them and turn them to your advantage.

A few weeks before writing this, I started a discussion on LinkedIn, asking what the top three killers of creativity were.

LinkedIn is great for keeping your finger on the pulse, because you can connect with a range of people who're in touch with the topic at hand. Being able to reach people from all over the world, from all different companies, who work with, lead, or are creative people, gives you fantastic insights. The answers you get can be surprising, but also current and relevant. It's a great way to see what's really going on and what your market really thinks.

It quickly became clear that certain patterns were appearing, the same creative killers popping up in different clothes. Having compiled everything, here's the top ten.

1. risk aversion
2. lack of structure (or the wrong structure)
3. time
4. not listening
5. status quo
6. my ideas are better than yours
7. unclear goals and poor briefs
8. lack of collaboration
9. micromanagement
10. lack of motivation

If you want to stop creativity in its tracks and kill the intangible beast, then here's the poison to do it with. But again, once things are known, you can steer away from them and protect your creative people from them. When you do, they will thrive.

So how do you make them thrive?

Let's take another angle. What motivates creatives? That's a different question. To get them really fired up, you need to hit the right buttons. We all know that you can't motivate anybody, no matter how hard you try — but you *can* help people achieve what's important to them. First, you need to know what that is.

Creative people are motivated by different things, so if you're going to lead them effectively, help them be their best and, in turn, use their talents fully, you need to understand what those motivations are.

1. self-fulfilment

2. recognition

3. being part of a team

4. artistic integrity (tie)

5. financial compensation (tie)

6. respect

7. career advancement

8. reward

This stuff is food for the intangible beast. In fact, it's a banquet. You can feed the beast sustenance and keep it alive, or you can indulge it and make it happy and productive.

It's an interesting list, because it varies from what corporate leaders think creative people need. But again, it's about helping creative people be their very best — so knowing what they desire and what they need is a huge advantage.

THE NUTSHELL

Undeniably, creativity has great value in the business world, but it's hard to pin down and feels intangible. Although we get the value it offers the world, we also recognise that we rarely make the most of that value.

And because of the intangible nature of creativity, we need to learn to understand it and accept it for what it is. If we try to define it, define who is and isn't creative, and how to do it, then we only end up destroying its potential.

If we can recognise what frustrates creative people (red rags) and what things businesses do that kills creativity (poison), we can then start working towards eliminating those things. And if we understand what motivates creative people (food), then we can provide the perfect diet to promote the very best creative health.

Bridging the creativity gap is a challenge. The answer lies in how well you lead and inspire your creative people and how you welcome and stimulate creativity in your business.

Let's move on to the most important creative resource your company has: people.

PART

TWO

PEOPLE

03: Who are the Creative People?

LABELLING CREATIVES

Just because someone can't paint doesn't mean they're not creative.

There is a great divide, an us-and-them scenario, when we talk about 'creative people'. As we discovered with the intangible beast, labelling certain people as 'creative' actually excludes others. By placing creatives into silos and defining who they are, we are once again limiting ourselves.

Because business leaders often have a narrow view of who the 'creatives' really are, they can't fully tap into the creative potential and wisdom of their organisation. I've sat in many brainstorming sessions and production meetings and I've always been amazed at how often the meek, mild, quiet person in the corner, who's not considered part of the creative team, comes up with the killer idea or adds a completely new twist to the conversation.

Part of the reason we place creative people into 'silos' comes from our perception of who the creative people are. Maybe at school we took art classes or music lessons and connected being creative with throwing paint around a room, or hitting a trance-like state as we practiced our musical scales. Maybe someone, somewhere, once told us that we weren't very creative and should focus on a more practical profession, such as engineering. Maybe we see creative people as those people working in advertising, fashion, and PR, or in engineering and IT. Maybe we once worked for a business where the creative team was segregated, that special group of people on Level 2 who did all the design work and advertising copy.

Just because someone can't paint doesn't mean they're not creative. Their creative talents may lie elsewhere and just because they don't fit the creative view of others or the creative personality of that industry doesn't mean they should be excluded.

As mentioned in Chapter 1, in June 2010 Fast Company released a special edition of 'The 100 Most Creative People in Business'. Within the list are people from a whole range of industries, not just the stereotypically creative ones such as advertising, fashion, and film. Yes, of course the list contains people from Google, Apple, Sony, and the likes, but it also contains people from IT, retail, finance, law, education, and even the fire department. Creative people are everywhere.

The us-and-them attitude basically comes down to your view of who a creative person is. My view is that a creative person is someone who thinks differently. To be creative is to create — whether it's a new concept, a new product, or a new idea. Being creative is about thinking and doing differently. It's about being unique, seeing the world from different perspectives, challenging the norm, and seeking possibilities.

A creative person is someone who thinks differently.

I'm not saying we should exclude, sack, or stop respecting our creative teams. Far from it: we need them. But we must beware of limiting our perceptions of who is and isn't creative. We need to broaden our view of who 'they' are and where 'they' are found. We need to stop thinking of creative people as 'those people in the corner with ponytails'. Even those outside your creative teams can and should contribute to your creative well-being.

Part of our job as leaders is to recognise that everyone has different creative strengths and they may be very constructive.

NON-CREATIVE BEHAVIOUR IS LEARNT

Most people don't actually believe they are very creative — but actually, you could say we unlearn to be creative as we go through life.

Let me introduce you to a gentleman by the name of George Land — an educator and author who did an experiment many years ago. He got hold of a creativity test from NASA and gave the test to a bunch of five year-old children. An astounding 98% scored as highly creative. Remarkable, isn't it?

The next part is even more remarkable. Five years later, he gave the test to the same children — now ten and having done the test before. This time, only 30% scored highly creative! In the short space of five years, the percentage dropped dramatically.

He then gave the test to a group of adults and only 2% scored highly creative. Yes, you read that right: 2%.

Does this mean we get less creative as we grow older? I don't believe it does. I believe that as we get older, we just don't *believe* we're very creative, because we don't know how, or we're out of practice, or we've had it knocked out of us.

This shows that we all have a natural ability to be creative which we lose as we move on in life. George Land himself concluded that 'non-creative behaviour is learnt'. Not the other way around.

Think about it. As we grow older, we gain more life experience, make more assumptions, take fewer creative risks, and tend to come up with ideas we think people *want* to hear rather than what we think they *should* hear. We play it safe. We come up with adequate ideas, but not truly creative ones.

Children have fewer inhibitions, ask more questions, and are far more inquisitive. They tend to be less afraid of ridicule. They don't make as many assumptions, they play and explore more than us, and they hang out in more stimulating and creative environments.

Does this mean we should become more childish in our creative endeavours and thinking? No. But in George Land's study lie many lessons and secrets to becoming a more creative business.

You need to help your people feel less inhibited and encourage them to ask questions, challenge things, and explore possibilities. Above all, you need to help them feel safe about being creative, speaking up, and throwing an idea on the table.

As leaders, we need to give our people permission to be creative. We need to be an inspiration to them and we need to protect them from having their creativity knocked out of them.

It's quite a responsibility and one you shouldn't take lightly.

We need to give our people permission to be creative.

I would venture to warn against too great an intimacy with artists as it is very seductive and a little dangerous.

—QUEEN VICTORIA

CREATIVE PEOPLE ARE EVERYWHERE

We all know that some people are definitely more creative than others (I will never be Pablo Picasso) and we should all be very grateful for it. That's why we have creative teams and creative departments, so we can tap into their talents and unique abilities.

But does that mean we should draw a figurative line in the figurative sand and decide who can and who can't creatively contribute to our business? Of course not. We shouldn't exclude everybody else and we certainly shouldn't limit who can be part of our creative teams.

THE CREATIVE SECTOR

At a recent breakfast meeting, someone whom I consider very creative asked what it meant to work in the creative sector. It's an interesting question, to which my answer was, 'Well... it depends.' Like all things creative, it depends on your point of view, your context, and what statistics you look at. Nothing is black and white.

Consider the quotation from Richard Florida in the first chapter: that the creative sector makes up nearly 30% of the workforce in the US. According to the Australian Bureau of Statistics in Australia, the creative sector makes up about 8% of the workforce — but I also have a report on my desk from the Queensland Government, which I cited earlier, stating that up to 35% of people are employed in creative industries in Australia.

If Australia limits its definition of 'creative' to a list of eight industries, does that mean people who work in events organising, engineering, or science aren't creative? Of course not. It only proves, once again, that defining stuff is dangerous. It all depends on how you look at it.

CREATIVE SECTORS

Creative people are everywhere, in all industries, across all sectors. To many of us, they mostly seem to hang out in design, marketing, fashion, or film. But do they? What about Atlassian? One of the best examples of a truly great creative company and they make software! What about J.A. Birchall from Tasmania, who owned a stationary shop? Inventing the writing notepad is a pretty creative endeavour. What about NASA? Getting a man on the moon and back again is pretty creative as well.

Remember the Tom Hanks film, *Apollo 13*? Tom and the boys in the Apollo spaceship are running out of air, because their CO_2 filter has died. A bunch of engineers are sitting around a table when the head guy wanders in, dumps a heap of stuff onto the table, and says, 'This is what they have up there and we need to figure out how to make a CO_2 filter out of it.' Taking up the challenge, the engineers get to work and figure out a solution. Those weren't "creatives" doing design or copywriting, they were engineers. So is that still creativity? Of course! In fact, some of the most creative people I know are engineers.

Some of the other most creative people I know are events organisers, producers, show directors, set designers — yet in Australia, the events industry is considered part of tourism, not the creative sector. I personally have very creative clients in IT, finance, and pharmaceuticals, as well as the classically defined 'creative' companies from the 'creative' sector, such as design and TV. Education hankers for more creative methods of teaching and for teaching to be more in line with creativity and the arts.

The truth is that creative people come in all shapes, sizes, and flavours, with a myriad different skills and abilities.

The truth is that creative people come in all shapes, sizes, and flavours, with a myriad different skills and abilities. They hang out in all different industries and professions from design to advertising to science to marketing to engineering, and the list is endless. They can be found everywhere. They're from all walks of life and can be found on every level of your organisation.

Creative people are everywhere.

THE HIDDEN CREATIVE

There are two types of creative people in every organisation: hidden and visible.

The visible ones are those you know are creative, because they're in your creative team. They do all your design and advertising work, develop your software. Perhaps they're contracted and part of your outsourced creative team. They studied their craft and they're constantly up-skilling themselves, developing, and exploring their talents. Being 'creative' is who they are and what they do, and it shows.

These are the designers, the IT engineers, the film-makers.

But who are the hidden creatives?

"In their book *The Disney Way* Bill Capodagli and Lynn Jackson tell of when Walt Disney was building his 'Pirates of the Caribbean' ride in Disneyland, he got his staff to have a ride and then comment back to him. One of his workers was from the Deep South (where, of course, the ride was set) and remarked that somehow the ride just didn't feel right. He couldn't quite put his finger on what it was.

Disney told him to keep riding it until he figured it out.

There's definitely an art to leading creative people.

Finally, the penny dropped. There were no fireflies in the bayou part of the ride, when you first got in the boats. It just didn't feel like the real Deep South. Now if you've ever gone on the 'Pirates' ride, you'll know what I'm talking about — those tiny lights above you as you meander peacefully through the waters ahead of the 'Dead men tell no tales' drop.

Here's the thing: part of Walt Disney's genius was his amazing ability to draw out the creative best from people. Yes, he surrounded himself with a creative team like no other (indeed, some of the most creative people of his time) but he also saw the value of tapping into *everyone*'s creative talents. There's great value in that.

There's definitely an art to leading creative people. Part of that art is to be open to and support the possibilities and ideas of those outside the 'creative camp'.

As a leader of creative people, you need to draw on and seek out the creative wisdom of others — to seek new perspectives. Don't be threatened by that; welcome it with open arms. Encourage your team to do the same. Seeking the creative input of others brings huge benefits. And if your creative team does the same, they'll open the doors to far greater input and ultimately greater possibilities.

And that pays dividends.

A friend I met at the Disney Institute, photographer Dennis Hodges, sent me a story on LinkedIn a while ago. I loved it so much I asked if I could quote it — so here it is.

Years ago, my family and I were sitting at breakfast at Disneyworld when an electrician walked through the dining room on his way to the kitchen area, presumably to repair something. As he passed our table, he stopped, reached into his tool belt, and produced a long balloon. After inflating it, he proceeded to create a balloon animal — Pluto, to be exact — handed it to my daughter, wished us a nice day, and proceeded onto his 'real' work.

I've reflected on this over the years as I've sat in meeting after meeting of financial types who are looking for the financial return on everything. How does Disney calculate that electrician's time to stop, probably several times a day, and tie balloon animals when his key task is to repair electrical problems? If he stops ten times a day and takes six minutes per stop, an hour of his work day is devoted to entertainment, not electricity.

The lesson for me is two-fold: one, that within this electrician lies a creative talent that 'gets it' when it comes to Disney's ultimate mission; and two, you can't always place a dollar amount on everything you do — even though the value of retelling this story over the years has to have a return for Disney in some fashion.

Thanks, Dennis. I appreciate it.

Every business has its hidden creatives. They can be anyone, anywhere. And we need to be open enough to seek them out and accept them.

THE RALLYING CRY

I have always had a passion for all things creative and all people creative. It's just how it is. I'm always stunned and delighted by the creativity in people. And I have an undying belief that people are far more creative then they give themselves credit for, and far more creative than others give them credit for.

The sad thing is that your organisation is crammed with creative people and you don't even know half of them are there. It's not just a waste: it's a creative crime. If we are truly to lead the creativity in our organisation, then we need to seek people out, inspire them to be more creative, and ask for their contributions.

THE NUTSHELL

Your creative team will always be at the heart of your organisation's creative potential — but by opening your view of who creative people are, you increase that potential and the size of the creative pool you can draw on. What's more, you'll enjoy a wider variety of viewpoints and greater possibilities. Imagine Disney's 'Pirates of the Caribbean' ride without the fireflies — a little bit of the magic would be lost.

That takes the right leadership. So let's take some time to talk about what it takes to be a great leader of creative people, to inspire and draw the creative best out of others.

Perhaps, instead of thinking about how to lead creative people, we should think about how to lead the creativity *in* people. And that's what the next chapter looks at: being the right leader.

04: Being the Right Leader

When you lead and inspire your people to be their creative best, when you support, nurture, and respect them, and know what drives or frustrates them, then the creativity gap closes naturally. Closing the gap isn't about things — it's about people. It isn't about doing stuff — it's about leading and inspiring people to be more creative. It's knowing how to help people be their creative best. The right leader of creative people understands that creative people think, feel, and do differently, and knows how to help them do just that. It's a different way of thinking and, as a result, a different way of leading.

Which is why it's not about finding creative people or teaching people to be more creative. Sure, those things need to be done, but they're not what will really set your business apart creatively and set the world on fire. Let's explore why.

Firstly, to increase their creative capital, business leaders usually put their efforts into *finding* creative people. They want to build a solid team of individuals or perhaps seek out creative 'rock stars'. That's fine — you need a great team of creative people around you and it's an area we'll revisit in the chapter on Casting. But finding creative people doesn't bridge the creativity gap.

Does this mean your people aren't important? Quite the opposite. They're vitally important and don't let anyone tell you otherwise. But actually, good creative people are everywhere.

They might be hard to find or track down, you might not have the resources to afford the 'rock stars', or you might have the wrong mix of skills, but you can fix those things quite easily. But even if you put together the best creative team (and you should aim for that), you still need to know how to lead them.

You need to deal with them and allow them to thrive. You need to get the most out of their talents and maintain their enthusiasm, then direct their talents towards obtaining commercially viable results. That's the art. Without great leadership, the world's best team will only go part way towards achieving your business success. And they want you to lead them and support them, so they can do what they do best — be creative.

Secondly, business leaders often focus on teaching their people to be more creative. Again, a worthy endeavour and one I'm all in favour of. (In fact, I conduct creativity workshops all over the world.) But actually, teaching your people to be more creative isn't hard. You can bring in experts to help your people think more creatively, take the team away for a creative retreat, or allocate resources for them to learn new skills and build on their talents. Constant learning should simply be a part of how you do things; it's vital to the creative success of your business. But even if you teach your people to think more creatively and bang out ideas endlessly, it doesn't bridge the creativity gap.

Leading creative people is like herding monkeys.

Both finding creative people and training their creativity are important when leading creative people. But neither of them is the main focus. What guides both those practices and what ensures you get the most out of your people and their skills is *knowing how to lead them and knowing how to inspire them.*

HERDING MONKEYS

Leading creative people is like herding monkeys.

Creatives seem to be all over the place, off in a world of their own. But they're also very communal and love hanging out with other creative types. They're brilliant at slinging stuff; they're always throwing ideas, designs, and concepts around. They love to play and explore, and they're very inquisitive. They're also incredibly smart. And you need them as much as they need you.

They think, feel, and act very differently, so you need to understand them — understand how they like to work, what frustrates and motivates them, how to protect them, what they want from you, and how to help them create their best. You need to know what drives them, what resources they need, what kind of community they want, and what values they cherish.

But in order to ensure their talents are directed towards your and your client's expectations and goals, you need to have and maintain a clear vision. They need to know what the task at hand is. Robert Davis of Davis Advertising Inc put this beautifully when he said, 'My job is to develop and communicate my vision.'

THE BLUNDERBUSS IS DEAD

The old-school style of leadership simply won't work with creative people.

You know the one, where you put on your pith helmet, grab a blunderbuss shotgun in one hand and a machete in the other, and head off into the jungle, crying 'Right-ho, lads, follow me!' You bombastically blaze a trail into the wilderness, your team loyally following right behind you. As you hack into the vegetation, your people are trampling over the narrow path you've made, making it a little more worn, a little more defined, until finally a new trail is furrowed into the deep, dark depths of the unknown. If your people are following directly behind you, then that's not creativity, it's conformity.

Sure, it may at first appear that you're inspiring others to be creative — after all, you're heading into No-Mans Land. That indicates exploring new territories, and being creative is all about exploring and discovering new things, right? But if all your people are simply lining up behind you, they're not being explorers and they're not being creative. One person is doing it and everyone else is re-doing it.

And just because you're blazing a trail into the wilderness doesn't mean you're going to end up in the right place. Many pitch-helmeted explorers got lost and many headed into the unknown never to return.

The blunderbuss is dead. Maybe it was okay last century, but it simply doesn't cut it for the twenty-first century. If you try leading creative people the blunderbuss way, they won't follow you and they won't play that game.

LONG LIVE THE PRODUCER

Leading creative people into the next part of this century requires more finesse. It's very much like being a Hollywood producer. Why? Because Hollywood is all about the business of creativity. It taps into the potential of exceptionally creative and clever people, and lets them do their thing, but it directs and funnels that potential to become commercially successful.

The last thing you want to be is their boss.

When we think of Hollywood, we often think of actors, directors, writers, and set designers, all of whom are immensely creative. They're the ones whose talents we see spring to life on screen — but there's another major player in Hollywood, whose job is focusing and steering that talent towards a successful outcome. The producer.

The producer's role is to bring the creative talents of those people together, let them do what they do best, and direct it so that the film pays dividends.

Like it or not, Hollywood is about making money from creative people. And you should like it: it allows many talented people to do what they love doing. Sure, you can train up your actors, directors, and set designers (and you should), but the key to getting business results is to orchestrate their talents and genius. It's important to build individual talents; it's absolutely crucial to build the right leadership skills, the right environment, and the right processes. That will allow your creative people to thrive, with all their creativity, thoughts, and ideas. That is where the future gold of your business resides.

Long live the producer! If you lead creative people this way, they'll thrive and love you, because you understand them, inspire them, help them be the best they can, and give them a reason to create something of value.

Perhaps we should change the word *lead* to *nurture, empower,* or *inspire,* and perhaps we should change the term *creative leader* to *creative producer.*

DON'T BE THE BOSS

To lead creative people effectively, you need to be a nurturer and custodian of their talents. You need to be a mentor and a coach. You need to know how to inspire them, empower them, guide them, earn their respect, and let them play. The *last* thing you want to be is their boss. Respect and encourage their creativity, protect them against the corporate stuff, and you'll get the best from their creativity — the creativity that your business needs in the new creative economy.

DON'T TELL THEM HOW TO DO SOMETHING

Creative people hate being told how to do something. When you think about it, it's condescending. The reason they exist in your business in the first place is because of their expertise and unique ability. So rocking up and telling them how to do their job is like telling a brain surgeon where to make the first incision. Most likely, the brain surgeon will tell you to take a jump as well.

#1 creative frustration: tell them how.

Clients are particularly good at doing this too. They often don't understand the creative process or how creative people work, so it's understandable. It's up to you, the leader, to act as a buffer and translate, acting with discretion.

Imagine you're standing on a mountain, telling your people that you need to get across the valley. Let them figure out how — that's what they do best. The role of the creative people's leader is to support and guide, not interfere or constrain. The 'blunderbuss' style of leadership — the 'Follow me!' style — is telling them *how*. But the leader standing on the mountain is telling them *what needs to be done*.

Think back to *Apollo 13*, when they're building a CO_2 filter out of whatever they had on board in space — the leader tells them *what*. Their whole challenge is the *how* — and that's what gets them going.

As Rob Goffee and Gareth Jones say in their book *Clever*, 'Tell them what — but not how.' They go on to add, 'Clever people don't need to be told — and generally don't want to be told — how to get something done. What they need is instruction on what they need to get done.'

Creative people love a challenge; they love being set a task. As leaders, you need to give them the *what*. Set the goal, the vision, the assignment, and the challenge — but let them figure out the *how*.

#9 creative killer: micro-management.

Micromanagement is strongly related to the first frustration of creative people — telling them how — but it's a step further in. More than telling them how, it's doing it for them. We've all had the experience of someone telling us how to do something and managing a project from over our shoulders — though surely none of us are guilty of that! While creative people love having clear direction and knowing what's required of them, they hate someone doing their job for them. Micromanaging tells your team you don't trust or respect them. It's insulting.

As soon as you tell a creative person how to do something, they'll switch off — so just give them the *what*. Direct them, steer them, guide them, and lead them, but whatever you do, stop micromanaging, don't tell them how to do their job, and don't start doing it for them!

RESPECT THEM

#2 creative frustration: don't respect them.

Creative people love to be respected for their talents and abilities. And they need to be told. If you ask a room full of creatives about the major frustrations they have working for organisations, lack of respect will inevitably come up.

Perhaps it stems from the intangible beast — viewing creatives as ponytailed, paint-throwing, bicycle-riding freaks. Or perhaps we don't appreciate the value they add to an organisation. Perhaps people simply don't understand the effort that goes into creating. Maybe it's the years of experience, training, endless mistakes, and failures creatives go through. It doesn't really matter why — a little respect goes a long way.

#6 creative motivator: respect.

Having respect is one thing; showing respect is quite another. You need to let them know. I'm not saying to swoon all over them or drool on their work, but let them know you appreciate them. Don't do it because you've read this; do it because you really do genuinely respect them.

One thing you must never do with creative people is act superior or above them. Although they understand and appreciate hierarchy and chain of command, they don't respect or like people throwing their weight around. Lead them, mentor them, guide them, and include them, but don't manage them or boss them about. Creative people are happy knowing someone's in charge and knowing what's required of them, but they also need your respect.

#9 creative frustration: act superior.

BE THEIR PROTECTOR

Remember in 'The Guide to Intangible-Beast Keeping', we spoke about what frustrates the intangible beast and what poisons it? You need to protect your creatives against the things that deaden or poison their creativity — red tape, bureaucracy, and long meetings.

#3 creative frustration: loads of red tape.

Creative people hate red-tape! As a creative person, if you need to fill in a 7d-9A form every time you want to book the editing suite, it will drive you to the brink of insanity — especially if there's no-one using it at the moment.

Creative people do understand and respect the need for order and systems — they just don't want to have to do it.

And it's not that creative people aren't good at detail. An editor is great with detail. But it's a different type of detail. It's a necessary, creative detail. Bureaucratic detail is a completely different kettle of fish and most creative types find it a total nuisance. And rightly so: if you have to constantly fill out forms and reports, it takes you away from your creative mindset and restricts the creative flow. If organisations bog you down in admin and bureaucracy, how are you meant to do the creative stuff?

So leaders need to do two things: streamline red-tape and act as a buffer against bureaucracy.

Being creative is about doing. It's proactive. Part of the process is pondering and musing on a problem, but what creative people really love is rolling up their sleeves and doing stuff.

In *Apollo 13*, the engineers got really turned on when the head guys gave them something to do: putting together piles of stuff from the spacecraft to make the CO_2 filter. It's not the talking, it's the doing that really gets creatives fired up.

Creative people like clear direction and they like boundaries, but briefings and meetings are a necessary evil. Schedule too many or make them too long, and your creative people will get irritated and turn off.

#10 creative frustration: lots of long meetings.

They also hate getting sucked into meetings that they don't actually need to be at. You need to be the buffer. Protect your people from these 'time-wasters' — even though they may not be time-wasters for your clients and stakeholders.

WIP (work-in-progress) meetings are terrific — if they're kept short, sharp, and relevant. (Oh boy, I don't want to *think* of the number of needless meetings I've sat in.) Make them short and to the point, involve coffee if it helps, keep them relevant, and do everything you can to lessen them.

When you streamline your red tape and processes, streamline your meetings as well. Just give the creatives what they need to know.

WHY THEY NEED YOU

Let's look at the role of a leader from a different perspective — from the point of view of a creative person. After all, there are lots of reasons why creative people want and need you as their leader.

The world is full of creative people who just want to create and are happy to just create for you.

One of the things creative people crave is the freedom to create: to push the boundaries, voice their ideas, and express themselves. They hanker for the creative freedom to pursue their talents, ideas, and passions. Working for the right organisation can help them achieve that. In fact, they often achieve it better than if they head off into the commercial wilderness on their own.

Freelancing doesn't always offer the creative freedom that you seek as a creative person. It brings a certain level of freedom, but also uncertainty and extra responsibility. That doesn't appeal to many or simply doesn't work for them. While some excel at the business side, many find great benefits in working for a business. And for many, having a stable place to head off to every day is a utopian ideal. Not having to worry about finding new clients, paying bills, or marketing your services offers the freedom to focus your talents on what you do best: being creative.

I want to put a ding in the Universe.

—STEVE JOBS

Success in freelancing doesn't guarantee creative freedom either. Once you get the hang of freelancing, the next logical step often seems to be building up your own business, then paying people to run and manage it for you. As a business owner, though, you step beyond 'freelancer'. And the process of building and maintaining a business can be daunting, ultimately taking you away from your creativity. Of course, some creative people are great at that side and relish it — a good friend of mine started her own design business and loves the business aspect of it. (In fact, her business, 2birds design group, created the design of this book.) Her focus has changed and that's fine as well. But plenty of others have no desire to take on a leadership role, because what really turns them on is being creative. And fair enough.

For many, once they step out of being a 'creative' and into being a 'freelancer' or 'business owner', the world of being a creative is never the same again.

Rocking up to work each day and working for somebody else has huge advantages for many people — including you, as a leader. Recognise it and be grateful that the world is full of creative people who just want to create and are happy to just create for you. In return, you need to give them the freedom they need to do that.

THE NUTSHELL

Leading creative people is like herding monkeys, because they think, feel, and act very differently, so the old 'blunderbuss' style of leadership simply doesn't work anymore. For the modern world, you need to be like the film producer: guide them, give them clear instruction about what needs to be accomplished, respect them, and protect them from bureaucracy.

The role of a leader of creative people is crucial. For many creative people, there are great advantages to working for your business. They need you as much as you need them.

So let's look at why that is and what motivates and drives your creative people.

05: What Motivates Creatives?

To lead creatives well, you need to understand what motivates them. There are good reasons why creative people like working for you, but what drives them? That's a different question.

#10 creative killer: lack of motivation.

Unsurprisingly, people find it hard to be creative if they're unmotivated. It's interesting that motivation came up in creative killers: it shows that many creative people aren't being motivated. If people aren't motivated, then they'll only do what's required, they'll give you adequate and competent results instead of brilliance, and very likely fade away and leave. That doesn't bridge the creativity gap; it broadens it.

You can't thrust motivation on anyone. You *can* help people achieve what's important to them — but first you need to know what that is.

Creative people are motivated by different things and those things vary from person to person. Find out what turns your creatives on and help them attain it. If you help them get what they want, they will help you get what you want.

CREATIVE MOTIVATORS

So what drives your creative people? Let's go back to the survey we conducted, where we asked that exact question of creatives. The Number One motivator was *self-fulfilment*, closely followed by *recognition* and then *being part of a creative team*.

#1 creative motivator: self-fulfilment.

TOP CREATIVE MOTIVATORS

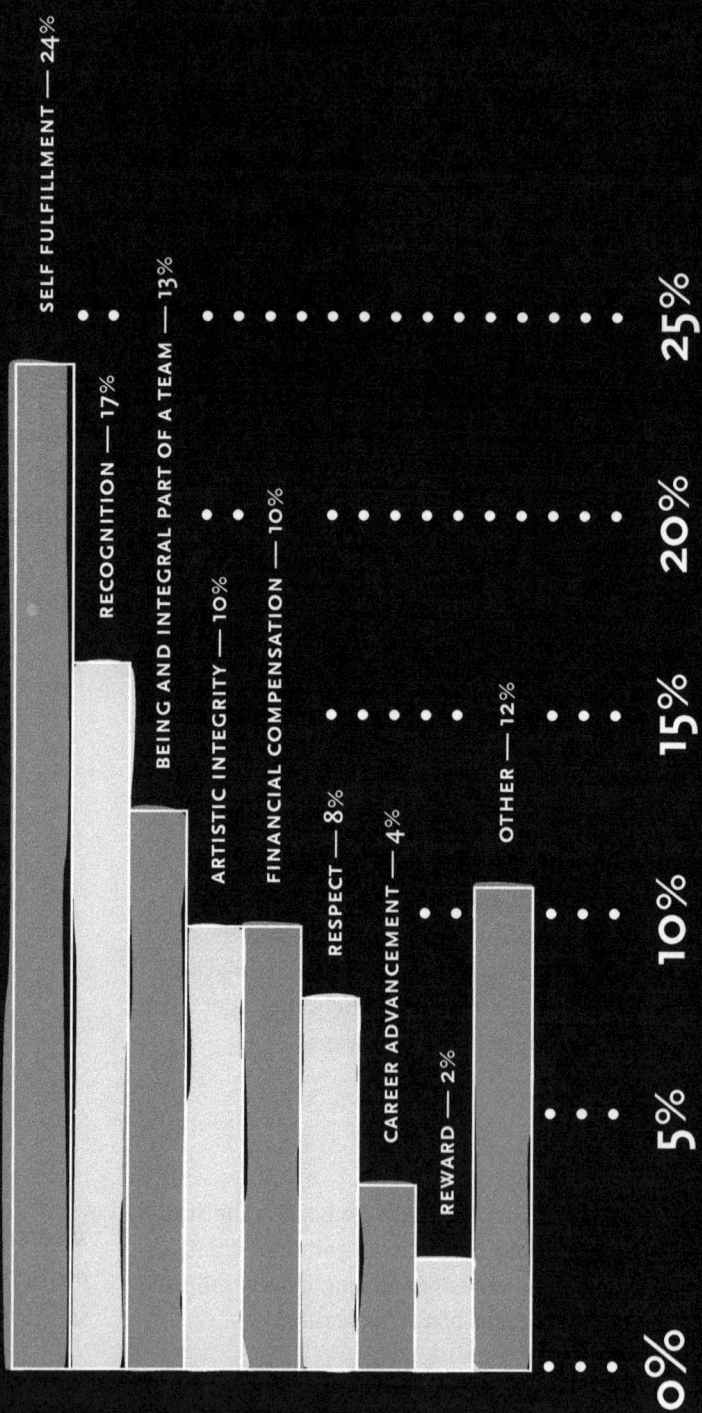

SELF FULFILLMENT — 24%

RECOGNITION — 17%

BEING AND INTEGRAL PART OF A TEAM — 13%

ARTISTIC INTEGRITY — 10%

FINANCIAL COMPENSATION — 10%

RESPECT — 8%

CAREER ADVANCEMENT — 4%

REWARD — 2%

OTHER — 12%

25%

20%

15%

10%

5%

0%

Importantly, financial compensation came in equal fifth, with only 10% listing it as their major choice. Money does matter, as we'll see, but it's rarely the top motivator. *Career advancement* was way down on the scale as well — which doesn't surprise me. As we saw, career advancement can mean less opportunity for creatives to do what they do.

So it's important to understand that what motivates you as a leader doesn't necessarily motivate your creatives. It's like trying to get your children to have bath by telling them it will make them clean. To a four year-old, there's nothing motivating about getting clean — that's your motivation. To a four year-old, it's quite the opposite: taking a bath is all about making a mess and splashing water all over the place. Same result. Different motivation.

We only listed eight choices, but we also allowed people to leave comments. A number of participants said that it was a combination of factors; others said it was such things as *creative freedom* and *making a difference* that motivated them. Here's a list of other motivators:

- solutions to business problems and opportunities

- making a difference

- adding adventure

- helping others

- creativity that works — results!

- success

- creating helpful work that everyone feels good about

- helping people see the world through new eyes

- running with ideas

- seeing a finished product being used effectively

- creative freedom

- using talents in full

- contribution

- having fun, for crying out loud

- leading my company to financial and moral success by applying creative solutions to business problems and opportunities

Creative people aren't all driven by the same thing. To get the results you need, you need to understand what motivates *your* creative people and help them get it, rather than giving them what you think they need.

That said, there are some things almost all creatives want, which help motivate them and help keep their creativity alive: resources, community, and values.

THE RESOURCE BOOM

It takes resources to be creative, find creative solutions, and make them happen — which is one of the reasons your creative people love you. They need the resources to make their dreams come true.

And resources come in all different forms.

TOOLS

You need to give your creative people the right tools to do their jobs. As Robyn Munro at Atlassian says, 'We give them [creative people] awesome resources to do their jobs with — fast computers, large monitors, comfy Aeron chairs. We keep the office well stocked with snacks and drinks, so that if they get in a creative groove, they can keep at it without going hungry or ducking out for food.'

One of the most significant benefits a creative person gets from working for a business is access to the right tools: the best equipment, the latest software and technology. Things they probably wouldn't get access to otherwise, because they couldn't afford it.

It sounds simplistic. It's so simple, in fact, that it's easily overlooked or discounted. I've learnt from first-hand experience that you need to provide the very best resources you can. But I've also learnt that sometimes it simply isn't possible, because budget or time constraints just don't allow it. That's how things are sometimes. But having the right tools of the trade allows your creatives to deliver not only the best quality of work, but also great efficiency.

If you have an editor cutting a corporate video and you can only give them a two year-old system that's a bit clunky and slow, then you can't expect the best output from them — in quality or time.

PROJECTS, CLIENTS, AND FUNDING

Let's talk money: nothing gets done without it. It's why a business exists. Remember that Hollywood is about making money.

If you worked in Hollywood, you'd be very grateful for that. The money allows you to play, create, work on projects, and pay your rent. Sure, people make art films, but without the big commercial blockbusters, the art films often don't get made. Even they need funding of some sort. And yes, A-list actors like George Clooney love to make art films — but it's the blockbusters that support them and allow them to do it. Without the money, everything stops.

For creative people, another advantage of working for a company is that projects get funded. They don't need to haggle or find venture capital, because the business does all that. They get access to business and creative opportunities they may never have had without the financial resources of the organisation.

Any marketing or sales person will tell you, it takes effort to find clients. For freelancers, it takes time and effort to find the clients you want to work with and who want to work with you, who have the need and the financial resources to allow you to play.

As one creative put it, in a survey we conducted, 'I like that I don't have to worry about the business side of things. I don't like "selling" myself or trying to drum up new clients and work.' Does this mean that creative people are generally lazy? Not at all — just that they have a different focus. They like doing what they do, not hunting business.

As a leader of creative people, you need to understand that most creatives don't want to lead others or be business managers. What they love is the creative side of their work.

On the topic of money, let's talk about income. Creatives usually value a stable and predictable income more than how much they make. A steady income stream takes away any uncertainty. With that taken care of, they can get on and create, without worrying about paying their rent or mortgage, or choosing an espresso coffee over instant.

#8 creative frustration: play the money game.

Income is a 'hygiene factor'. If you don't take care of a cut, it gets irritating and begins to fester. Then you have a problem, and an annoying one, which stops you doing things and being yourself on a day to day basis. It's a graphic analogy, but you get the picture. A cut isn't a big deal — but if you ignore the hygiene factor, it can be a disaster. Income is important to creatives, but it's not the main thing — unless you ignore it.

#5 creative motivator: financial compensation.

That doesn't mean they don't know what they're worth: they like getting paid and they like getting paid well. Joris Luijke, Global Director of Human Resources from Atlassian believes they pay their creatives better than most, if not all, within the industry. That attracts and keeps good people. They don't pay bonuses to their people for high achievement either — they increase their salary instead. It has a more lasting effect. At my entertainment business, Absurd Entertainment, we paid our performers well — sometimes more than they quoted us, if we had the budget or knew it would be a tough gig. I always looked on that as good insurance. Plus, coming from an entertainment background, I genuinely appreciated our team's talent and spirit. Sometimes you just need to do things because it feels right and to hell with the reasons.

Pay your creatives well and pay them consistently.

Pay your creatives well and pay them consistently.

Money isn't a major driver, just something that needs to be taken care of, but it becomes a major frustration if you start playing games. Financially, you'll only upset things. Remember — it's a hygiene factor. Keep it clean, and it never becomes a problem.

COMMUNITY

Right from prehistoric times, people have always been very social beings. We like to share stories and experiences, we like being inspired by and inspiring others, and we like feeling that we're needed, that we're not alone.

#3 creative motivator: being part of a team.

Creatively, that's a huge advantage. When we asked what creative people like most about working for an organisation, the biggest response was the community. Creative people like hanging out with other creative people. It gives us a sense of belonging, being part of something bigger, being part of the team.

This was a crucial part of Absurd Entertainment. Absurd was a creative entertainment design company in the corporate events industry — which means it created and designed entertainment to suit the needs of individual projects and clients. So we needed to attract and maintain the right group of people to work with.

Astonishingly, we were the only entertainment company on the block to send Christmas cards to our performers. Not just standard 'Have a great Christmas' cards, but genuine hand-written notes of thanks and appreciation.

Why? Firstly, we really did appreciate the efforts our performers took to make things happen. That was important for us and our clients. Our mission as a company was 'to amaze people' and that takes effort, diligence, and commitment from the performers.

But we also wanted our performers to feel part of the team and the family. And that created a team of performers who were loyal and committed to Absurd. It was common for a performer to take one of our jobs over one of our competitors'. It was normal for performers to just drop by the office to say 'Hi,' when they weren't pitching for work. And when the going got tough and we needed our performers to go beyond what was expected, it was never an issue.

Even though we didn't employ our performers, we contracted them in on a per-job basis, they felt part of the community of Absurd.

As smart leaders, we want to embrace all of that — and we want to encourage and enhance it. Why? Because community means collaboration, developing new skills, and creating a place where your creatives want to hang out.

CO-OPERATION AND COLLABORATION

#5 creative frustration: segregate them.

Creative people love hanging out with other creative people. That's one of the reasons working with them is like herding monkeys. It stimulates them, stimulates collaboration, and allows them to bounce ideas around.

Being with like-minded people is incredibly stimulating and engaging. Conversations spark interest and open all sorts of doorways to new arenas of thought and interest. And it also makes good creative sense.

Creative people love hanging out with other creative people.

Working with a team allows creative people to get different perspectives on things. We each see the world differently, so hanging out with other people triggers fresh insights. It allows creative people to play to their strengths and tap into the strengths of others. It allows them to learn from each other and so grow their own skills.

It creates and promotes collaboration. It allows us to bounce ideas around, to check them, and to get input. Challenges and questions can be placed on the table in a friendly, respectful manner. It's wonderful.

So whatever you do, make sure your creative people get to network and hang out with others. Work out ways to help your creatives build networks, blow off creative steam, and develop sounding boards and avenues of inspiration.

8 creative killer: lack of collaboration.

But here's the caveat. Collaboration isn't just about hanging out in your own business: creatives also need to hang out with creative people from other businesses and other industries.

Tapping into the creative wisdom and talents of others is a major creative tool — but collaboration often gets restricted to the creative team or project team. Businesses are great at getting the people together *within* teams to bang out solutions, but the collaborative action stops there.

That gets back to putting creatives in silos. It's one thing to collaborate within a creative team and another altogether to collaborate with people outside the team, even outside the company and the industry. That's when you start getting really interesting input and ideas.

They also need to hang out with people whose main focus *isn't* creativity. That gives them a larger view of the world, new perspectives, and helps them get into the heads of other people from other worlds.

This isn't just good for business; it's good for the soul. Sometimes you just need to play: empty your head and have an outlet other then work. Don't leave that for people to do for themselves. It should be on the blueprint of building your creative human capital. Make sure you create opportunities for these things to happen.

Break down the us-and-them mentality between creatives and everybody else. Find ways to collaborate, not just inside but outside the camp. Nurture a culture of collaboration. That doesn't just happen — it takes effort and planning. In return, their collective creativity takes a huge leap forward and they learn new skills.

NEW SKILLS

Creative people need to learn new skills. That's true for everyone, of course, but creatives constantly hanker to try new things. It stimulates curiosity and combats boredom.

#7 creative frustration: contain their expertise.

Allow your creative people to follow that hankering — let them attend courses and seminars, visit places of interest to them, or just hang out with other people with different skills, so they learn how to do new things. Part of a community is sharing skills — don't restrict their skills to their job role, or you'll starve their creativity. And don't be too concerned if it's not industry or job-related, because it all adds up. The best inspiration often comes from outside the camp.

SPACE TO PLAY

It's essential to create an environment and culture that allows creative people to explore, play, investigate, and do all those things creative people need to do. If you have a workplace that works against that, then you're on the back foot. This is crucial and we'll explore it in detail in the next book, *Creating Zoos*. For now, let's take a quick look at the two key ideas.

Part of having space to play is about the actual physical space. Your physical environment affects your mindset dramatically, so having the right physical space is vital. That doesn't mean you need surreal rooms full of beanbags. It *does* mean you need a space conducive to being creative. One that welcomes and stimulates creativity, where creatives like hanging out and bouncing ideas around with each other. Where they don't feel inhibited or closed in, but free to let their creativity flourish.

Giving creatives space is also about the culture. Creative people like working for you if you give them the right environment, where they have the space and time to let the creative process do its thing — where the intangible beast can do its thing. They need to know they have a place where it's safe to be creative and where it is encouraged. The community needs to offer an environment that's conducive, both physically and mentally, to playing.

IT'S A TWO-WAY STREET

Remember: you are part of this community, too. You need your creative people as much as they need you.

Sadly, businesses sometimes view things as a one-way street. There's this attitude of 'They need me,' and 'I'm doing them a favour.' (If you've read this far, you probably don't have that view, but it's frighteningly common.) However, if you get the value proposition of creativity, and if you accept that the secret to unlocking its wealth lies in creative people, then you must also accept the fact that you need them.

By exploring why creatives like working for organisations, you can then know what and how to deliver. If you give your creative people what they need they will give you what you need.

THE 'VALUES' PROPOSITION

It goes beyond collaboration — community has a sense of
belonging to it. It's about looking out for each other, growing,
and moving forward together. We gain huge personal satisfaction
when we feel we've contributed to a higher cause, created
something together, and been part of something bigger than
us. As one creative put it, 'There is power in the co-operative
as well. Yelling from the mountaintop into the wind doesn't
always do it for me. I would rather have made a difference.'

*#4 creative
motivator:
artistic
integrity.*

Let's explore the importance of values to the creative well-being
of your business.

If everyone within an organisation is on the same page, working
towards the same things, aligned in their purpose, it creates
harmony and strength. Values are powerful things: they define
a company. You can have the best creative people working with
you, but if their values aren't aligned, it only creates drag as you
move forward. Get it right, and it creates momentum.

As Joanna Maxwell, a creativity coach, views it, 'In one sense,
values provide the ballast to ground creativity and give it depth.
Values are also the rudder, the sense of focus and direction that
increase the chance of a useful and practical outcome for the
creative activity.'

Nice.

Values are like a turbo charge, both for helping people take
ownership and in casting the right people. They add a bit of
extra fuel to the mix and create extra 'oomph'. Let's look at the
potential of 'the values turbo charge'.

VALUES ARE INTRINSIC

As you walk into the reception area of Atlassian in Sydney,
one thing that strikes you is the meeting room to your right.
Lots of businesses have meeting rooms off their reception
areas, but this one has big blue letters all over one of the glass
walls and these letters spell out the five values Atlassian has as
a company:

1. Open company, no bullshit

2. Build with heart and balance

3. Don't #@!% the customer

4. Play, as a team

5. Be the change you seek

I find that really impressive: these values aren't just something the company founders came up with because they thought they should. Their values are intrinsically linked to who the company and its people are and what they stand for.

When you visit their website, the values are listed for all to see — they're not for internal eyes only. Scroll down and you'll find a short video addressing what the values are and how they came to be. In it, they say, 'We looked at the company when it was much smaller and we looked at the things that made us do what we wanted to do. Which was build great products. And [then] we really looked inside and tried to figure out why it was we came to work each day. And [we] wrote down those reasons.'

The values Atlassian lives by aren't just something *created* in a moment of grandeur, an admirable add-on. Atlassian *identified* what the company stood for in its infancy. Michael Henderson, a corporate anthropologist, said, 'It seems to be that Atlassian have distinguished themselves from organisations that attempt to embody a set of values in a genuine manner. Atlassian have not created a set of values and then set out to live them. They have set out to be successful and then identified which values they have lived to enable them to achieve this. It's a simple, smart, and very effective use of values, one that many companies would be wise to copy. It's why they can be confident they are unlikely to lose sight of these values as they grow further.' That's important.

VALUES ARE SHARED

It's one thing to have a set of values, another to have people within the organisation owning those values. Businesses give values a lot of lip-service, but not at Atlassian. It's genuine and when you talk to the people there, it's clear: to them, these values are not just a list of cool ideas on a wall; they live and breathe them. The values guide them and are part of the very DNA of the company.

When values are clear,
decisions are easy.

—ROY DISNEY

As Robyn Munro wrote on her blog, 'I often talk about Atlassian's values to people outside the company, and the most frequent question asked is, "Are they real values that people live, or are they just words?" This is closely followed by, "How do you get people to follow them?"... It's important to state that we didn't create the core values, we just articulated values that the company and the staff were already living.'

Having sat with Robyn over many coffees, it's obvious that she not only agrees with them but also believes in what they stand for. That's powerful: if everyone within an organisation is on the same page and working towards the same things, then everyone is happy, coherent, and focused.

I asked Robyn about job interviews in the meeting room, with the values written loudly on the walls. How did people react to them? Her answer was that people usually loved them — that was why they were there for the interview in the first place. Most people loved the values and agreed with them. That means Atlassian's values attract the type of people Atlassian wants and the type of people who want to be there.

VALUES ARE SINCERE

A few years back at the Disney Institute in Orlando, a similar story unfolded for me. Everywhere I went, everyone I spoke to had the same drive, the same outlook, and the same attitude. Everyone was happy to be there and be part of the Disney experience. More importantly, it seemed that everyone was also concerned with my happiness. If you've ever been to Disneyland, you'll know what I'm talking about. It's just part of who they are and the way they do things.

Here's the thing that's blown me away every time I've been there: when someone at Disney says to you, 'Have a nice day,' they aren't just saying it because they have to or giving it lip-service. They genuinely mean it. It may get a tad annoying, but it's always said with courtesy and with the customer in mind. You can't help but enjoy it and be affected by it. They genuinely want you to have a great time.

How do you do that? How do you get everyone to align with that and take ownership of it? You do it by having really strong values, so people understand them, get their true meaning, can decide if they believe them or not, and then live by them and make them a part of what drives them and focuses their actions. Anyone who doesn't hold those values simply doesn't fit.

Disney is a very value-driven company. It always has been. It's part of the way Walt set it up, because he believed in what he and the company stood for, and he knew it was important to maintain those values in everything Disney did. Their 'Legacy' training program teaches new employees the values and culture of the company. That's powerful — it defines a company and guides everything they do.

VALUES ARE ALTRUISTIC

Atlassian's values include a couple of things they do which aren't for gain, but which do have great benefit.

One of these is called the Atlassian Foundation. Each year, 1% of company and employee time, 1% of company equity (not profit), and 1% of products are given to non-profit groups, donated or allocated in various ways to improve society and the environment. It's a great innovation and contributes a lot to the world.

People will choose to work for an inspiring business over one which simply requires them to do their job.

The other is Room To Read — a charity to which Atlassian donates the revenue from its start-up licenses. Basically, you can get started with an Atlassian product license for just $10 and the funds go directly to the charity. It's a great cause and it's also smart business, because it helps them capture the bottom end of the market. This initiative alone has raised over $1,000,000 in less than 2 years.

To me, those two things are impressive and worthwhile in themselves. But putting on my 'What's in it for the business?' hat and looking for the payoff, it means that people are inspired by it. I find it inspiring. It's good for clients, because they feel they are contributing to worthy causes and getting a great product at the same time. It's a great driver for attracting and retaining great people as Joris Luijke indicated — people will choose to work for an inspiring business over one which simply requires them to do their job and nothing more.

Through the Foundation and Room To Read, Atlassian offers a whole new level of involvement, pride, and empowerment. It offers a bigger picture and the chance of being part of the greater good. And that, quite simply, turns people on.

THE NUTSHELL

The fact that you need to know what motivates people to help them succeed is by no means a new notion. However, when it comes to creative people, they are motivated by different things. As a leader, you need to find out what *really* drives your creatives.

For many creative people, working for an organisation has enormous benefits. It can provide them with the tools, resources, projects, clients, and budgets that they need to do they were put on this earth to do — be creative. A business also gives them the sense of community they enjoy and allows them to develop their skills as well as acquire new ones.

Remember: it's a two way street. They need you as much as you need them.

And then to turbo charge their drive, add genuine values into the mix, because it's vital that the team is on the same page, working towards the same purpose — otherwise you have a bunch of creative people but not a coherent team.

Values give clarity, direction, and purpose; creative people like that. As Joanna Maxwell of Working in Colour says, 'Without values, there is no clear framework and so it's quite likely that random chaos will be the only noticeable outcome.'

So let's move on now and start bringing together both the people side and leader side to get results. From here, it's about creating a synergy between the two and driving it towards commercial outcomes. Remember the Hollywood producer? Their true ability is in combining their skills as leader with the talents of creative people to pay the dividends which the suits (the money people, the studio heads — or in your case, the stakeholders and clients) require.

PART

THREE

IN PRACTICE

o6: **Casting**

In the previous part, we looked at who creative people are and what motivates them. Now let's talk about pulling together the right team, for a particular project or for your business as a whole. That's important, because it's your team who are going to drive your business and get the results you need. If you get the wrong team in place, it just makes life harder and your projects become an up-hill battle. Getting the right team in place makes life so much easier — everything just seems to fall into place.

You need the best-right mix — not just the best people, or just the right people, but the best-right blend of skills, personality, and diversity. To do this, it helps to understand the four creative behaviours, so that everyone and everything is aligned and on the same page. When you bring people on board, you need to make sure they are the right fit, that they are the people you want, and that they are people who want to be there. Whether it's employing people or contracting freelancers, you need to have the very best team.

THE BEST-RIGHT MIX

BEST *and* RIGHT

From my experience of working on large events, getting
the team right was paramount. You can have the best talent
available in your team, pay them a fortune, and of course you
will get results. But if there are any *prima donnas* in the mix
or if they don't get on with each other (which often happens,
especially when you have a room full of creative stars who are
fiery and opinionated), then you get personality clashes, bad
energy flying around, and disharmony. Yes, it sounds dramatic,
but I've seen it, been in the thick of it, and it ain't pretty.
If your team doesn't cohere or is not aligned with each other
and with your overall vision and values, then you're not going
to get 100% out of them.

It's not about getting the best people or the right people; it's about getting the right, best people on board

You can also put together a team of the right people. By that,
I mean people who love what they do, take ownership, and are
aligned to your vision and values. And again, of course you will
get results. But if they lack expertise and star quality in their
work, then as a team they won't be as punchy and effective
as they could be.

It's not about getting the best people or the right people; it's
about getting the right, best people on board — or the best,
right people. In other words, it's getting the right *mix* of the
best people and the right people.

When you get a team of highly creative people together *and*
it's the right mix of highly creative people, that is a wonderful,
beautiful thing. Not only do you get amazing work, but you
also get harmony and drive. You get alignment in everyone
working towards achieving the same goals, to create something
bigger than them. (Remember, creatives like that.) To put it
in very plain language — when you get the best-right people,
it just rocks.

So you need to get the mix right. And the mix needs to work
on several levels.

SKILLS

Firstly, you've got to have the right mix of talents. That's almost a given, but you need to have the *right* people with the skills you need. For example, if you're a staging company which creates sets for films, events, and theatre, then there's no use having a team of outstanding set designers if you don't have an outstanding construction team to build them.

Putting a team together is like casting a film and putting the crew together. You need people with unique expertise from a range of different specificities: lighting, sound, cinematography, script-writing, acting, directing. You need to cover the skills bases.

PERSONALITIES

But you also want a team who get on well. If you're stuck on a deserted island for three months filming with a small group of people, you want to make sure that the group get on.

You need to have the right mix of personalities, people who are going to work well together. That's not to say they should spend each day hugging each other and agreeing about everything — you want the odd maverick to keep things provocative, as long as everyone's cool with it. But you need a group who respect each other for their talents and their work, and are open to each other's views, opinions, and maverickness.

DIVERSITY

*It's all in
the casting.*

And lastly, you want a diverse group of people to keep it interesting and offer their unique spin on things. Diversity isn't just skills-based — it runs across all kinds of areas, such as background, education, gender, and age. Creatively, the more you mix it up, the more unique perspectives and fresh input you're going to get. If your team are all from the same background and industry, how can you possibly expect a diverse range of ideas and solutions?

It's all in the casting.

THE FOUR CREATIVE BEHAVIOURS

Let's look at casting from a slightly different angle. If it's a matter of getting the mix right, then we also need to understand that creative people have different strengths, quite apart from their different skills and expertise. There are four different creative behaviours.

Take a circle and divide it into four with a horizontal and a vertical axis. Each of the four different behaviours falls into a quadrant.

The vertical axis represents activity — low at the bottom, high at the top. If you're sitting at the bottom of this axis, you have a low level of activity. In other words, you don't get much done. That doesn't mean you're lazy; it just means you're not an implementer. If you're at the top of this axis, you're fantastic at getting things done — you're the right person to give stuff to if you want it implemented.

The horizontal axis represents ideas — low on the left, high on the right. So if you're on the left of it, you're not great at coming up with ideas — which is fine, as well. If you're on the right, it means you can really crank the ideas out.

But people don't fall exactly on the axis — they hover in the quadrants, which gives us the four behaviours.

Note that these are different creative *behaviours*, not different creative *people*. Rarely do you or your team sit completely and totally in one position. You tend to flip about at different times and with different projects. You might find some members of your team are better at coming up with the ideas on certain projects and better at getting stuff done on others. Maybe it's because they're more familiar with the context or material. Maybe it's down to time constraints or the level of ownership they have on one project compared to another. Maybe it's just their level of expertise in that context.

So let's look at the four creative behaviours.

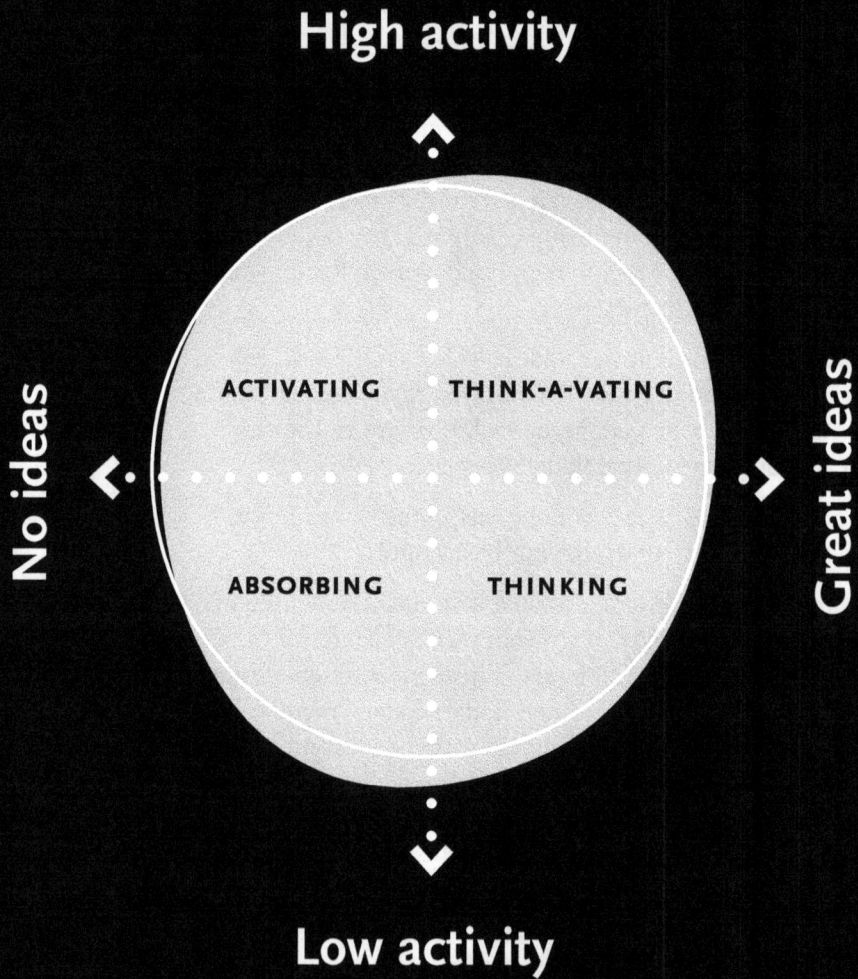

High activity

No ideas

ACTIVATING   THINK-A-VATING

ABSORBING   THINKING

Great ideas

Low activity

ACTIVATING

When people are in the top left quadrant, they're great at taking action. They may not be great at coming up with the ideas, but they'll get active and make them happen. In fact, quite often, ideas are passed to them, usually by the thinkers. We need people to do this, because they get ideas up and running.

This behaviour is called 'Activating'.

THINKING

When people are diagonally opposite, in the bottom right quadrant, they are fantastic at coming up with ideas and concepts. They're great at seeing possibilities. But in this quadrant, they're not very good at acting on those ideas. They're doing the ideas thing, but their challenge is to find a place in the world for their ideas. We need people to do this because we need great ideas; we need people to see unique and fresh possibilities.

This behaviour is called 'Thinking'.

ABSORBING

When people are in the bottom left quadrant, they're not coming up with ideas or acting on them. This doesn't mean they're less creative than everyone else — it means they're absorbing what's going on and usually they will end up contributing later on, often in amazing ways.

There are two reasons people will be absorbing. The first is that they are learning. This might be someone at the beginning of their career who's inexperienced, hasn't been given the right opportunities, or hasn't been taught how to use their creative talents. We need these people, because they are the future if we nurture them well. Alternately, they might be learning because they have a wealth of creative experience, but from from a different skill set; they may not have the experience on a particular project you've brought them into. Remember that learning new skills motivates people's creativity. It's part of your role as leader to help them do that.

The second reason for people absorbing is that they are observing. Creative people need to recharge their creative minds and hit the reset button from time to time. Extended periods of intense creativity can wear you down, which is why creative people often seem to be resting or doing nothing. Actually, during this time they are often observing, consciously or otherwise, taking things in, and letting them gestate. Alternately, sometimes they have taken a conscious decision to step back and watch what's going on – perhaps to give themselves a new and fresh perspective or perhaps to allow other people's ideas a chance to come to the fore.

Observers are the ones who just sit and watch, saying nothing until the time is right – then they often contribute great moments of wisdom and insight. Their added distance can also keep a project on track, by avoiding "group think" and helping to keep a helicopter perspective.

Whatever people's reasons for absorbing, this is an important part of a project's development *and* your team's development.

This behaviour is called 'Absorbing'.

THINK-A-VATING

When people are in the top right quadrant, they are really creative and good at coming up with ideas, and *also* fantastic at taking action on their ideas. This is gold. Think-a-vators are good at doing both things in a complementary manner. When someone is in this quadrant, they have a knack for finding the right ideas and making them work.

This behaviour is called 'Think-a-vating'.

ALL FOR ONE

#8 creative motivator: career advancement.

So on the surface, it may seem that the ultimate goal is to nurture and inspire your people to become think-a-vators. But not so.

The reality is that if all your people end up with think-a-vator behaviour only, then they won't be challenged and they'll end up going mad from boredom. Think of it like this: creatives love being challenged, it's in their nature, so if they are constantly brilliant at coming up with ideas and also at executing them,

You will do foolish things, but do them with enthusiasm.

— SIDONIE GABRIELLE COLETTE

then where's the challenge? It's all too easy. Sure, they will wander into that quadrant from time to time, maybe for an entire project, but if they stay there permanently they will become uninspired.

It's like learning to play guitar. If you learn to play a dozen songs really well, but that's all you ever play, you will get bored, put down your guitar, and maybe never pick it up again. You need to learn new songs, more difficult songs, to keep yourself interested and to keep elevating your skills.

So the goal then becomes having think-a-vator behaviour *as a team*, not necessarily as individuals within the team.

When we're putting together a creative team, it's important to understand that there's a blend of creative behaviours across all quadrants, and we need them all. We need people to think and provoke ideas, we need people to activate and get things done, and we need people who're learning, for their fresh perspectives and to develop their skills. Otherwise, you end up with a lot of uninspired, unchallenged, and bored creatives.

If you get the blend of creative behaviours right — if you get the casting right — the team itself becomes a 'think-a-vator'.

SELECTING YOUR PEOPLE

So how do you match up all those factors — the skills, personalities, diversity, and the right mix of behaviours? You need to be aware of these things and you need to think about them. But once you've done that, you also need to trust your instincts. Look for the right 'fit', recruit creatively, and pull your freelancers into the fold.

CASTING STUDIOS — LOOK FOR THE RIGHT FIT

If you've ever had the opportunity to sit in on the casting of a TV commercial, a corporate video, or a film, you'll have had a unique and fascinating experience. When you cast a film or a show, there are so many elements you're looking for besides sheer talent. You're not just looking for the skill level, you're also looking for how that person fits the brief and how their potential fits with the team.

Imagine this: as the director of a video, you need to find the perfect presenter to get your message across. You hire a casting director, they narrow the field down (much like a recruiter), and have a schedule of talent (actors and presenters) who will show up to be auditioned.

You call the first person into the room. It starts with a bit of chit-chat, some handshaking, and you thank them for coming. Part of your job is to help them relax. I've been on both sides of casting sessions, behind and in front of the camera, and for the person going for the job it can be a nerve-wracking and daunting experience — much like a job interview.

You may not realise it consciously, but you actually begin casting them as soon as they walk through the door: the way they stand, the genuineness of their smile, their energy. It's amazing how easily people start to fit your perception of who the right person is — but after all, you know your business, the message you want to convey, and your audience.

There is so much more to casting than finding the best talent.

Then the presenter steps in front of the camera and you ask a few simple questions, such as 'Name?' 'Agent?' and 'Tell us a bit about yourself.' Already, you're starting to get a feel for how they come across and whether they fit the brief.

Next, you ask them to present a portion of the script. At that point, you pretty much get a feel for whether or not they've got what it takes to win the gig. It's here that you really get to see what they're made of — not just their talent, but their confidence, openness to direction, manner, sincerity, and ability to really connect with the audience, your clients.

As the day progresses and you audition more and more presenters, it becomes clear that some really fit the brief and others just don't. For the ones who stand out, it goes way beyond their talent and ability. Sure, talent has to be right up there, but it's not the only consideration that will land them the job.

At the end of the day, you're down to two or three candidates. Each one is talented, but not necessarily more than the ones who didn't make it. What gets you is the fit. They just feel right for the shoot. Something about them screams that they are aligned with your business, your objectives, your beliefs, and your values.

There is so much more to casting than finding the best talent.

Let's visit our friends at Atlassian again, because they do some really smart things to get the right mix of the best and right people.

To Atlassian, their people are vitally important and they strive to get the very best in the industry — and then they strive to keep them. As Robyn Munro commented, 'Our staff are very happy working with us. We like to say that you work with Atlassian, instead of for Atlassian.' People are crucial to Atlassian and they pride themselves on attracting and keeping the best talent in the software business.

A while back, Atlassian put in place an initiative for a recruitment drive to 'find 32 of the best and brightest people'. They created some very clever approaches to achieve their goal. Again, in line with the open philosophy of Atlassian, you can find details on their website.

Here's how it worked.

Atlassian offered new employees a 'start fresh' initiative. Basically, this meant that before a new recruit began work, they were encouraged to take a few days off so they were fresh on their first day. Joris Luijke states in one of his blogs that they gave 'new hires a 'Wotif' voucher (up to $1k) to relax in a nice hotel!' That was an investment, but allowed new talent to be relaxed before they got there. Which is pretty attractive.

They also offered their existing staff a recruitment bonus of $10,000 to refer a friend to Atlassian, as an incentive to finding great people. Rather than paying recruitment companies the big bucks, they would rather pay their staff (which makes sense). Their staff tend to know the good people, because creative and talented people hang out with other creative and talented people. So not only do they get a direct pipeline to the best and most appropriate people, they reward their staff and save money at the same time. They also offered an external referral bonus of $2000 for people outside of Atlassian, which they called the 'refer-a-mate' program — again, pretty impressive.

It's a win-win-win. A win for Atlassian, a win for referees, and a win for new recruits. What's more, they're not just waiting for people to answer their ads – they're actively seeking out the people *they* want. That's smart.

Atlassian also opened up recruiting to recruitment companies, but did so on their terms. In fact they put three rules in place.

Firstly, when the first-time recruitment companies put forward candidates, they could only send a maximum of four. Recruitment companies weren't likely to send average candidates; they would need to send the best. That led to the next rule: if one of the four candidates submitted was hired, then the recruitment company was allowed to send more and become a recruitment partner. Finally, if none of the four were hired, the game was over. They didn't get another chance.

That might sound tough, but if you hold people as your Number One resource and you aspire to create the very best team you possibly can, then it's a fair call. As Joris says on his blog, 'It caused quite a stir.' But as far as casting goes, the payoff was huge.

Put those three things together and what was the result? Some pretty significant statistics, again listed on the Atlassian website. They almost halved their recruitment costs. That's enormous, especially when you think about the quality of new people they managed to attract. A significant reason for this was that internal referrals almost tripled, thanks to their 'refer-a-mate' program. At the same time, their hirers from recruiters went from 26% down to 4%. They also saw an increase of 350% in applications.

Do you think Atlassian have trouble getting hold of good people? No, they don't. They've created a demand in the industry — the right skills, diversity, alignment with their values, and quality. It means they can choose the best, right people.

That's a smart way of building the right team of talented and creative people. It demonstrates again the creative and innovative nature of Atlassian as a company. It shows they are an agile organisation who do things differently and are solutions-driven. Apart from putting their competitors on edge and letting the world know they were growing in a tough environment, they attracted the very best creative talent in the industry.

When you bring people into the team or the business, look the way you want for the people you want. That way, you get the best, right people, who share your values.

INVOLVE YOUR FREELANCERS

I've always believed that freelancers should be brought into the fold as much as anyone else, especially for project-based work. Freelancing has lots of advantages for a creative and for a business contracting freelancers. For a creative, it gives them freedom, variety, and control over their destiny and the jobs they choose. For a business, it brings an outside perspective, exclusive expertise, and often cost benefits.

But how do you gain the same level of commitment and ownership from a freelancer?

The answer to that is probably best illustrated through two examples, both from the events industry. The first comes from a business events producer, Ian Stewart, and the second from my own experience.

FREELANCERS ARE FOR LIFE, NOT JUST CHRISTMAS

Freelancers are for life, not just Christmas.

In Australia, Ian Stewart is highly respected and revered in the industry, and for the past thirty odd years has been one of the major players. I asked him what it took to deal with creative people, to get the most from them, but still hit the objectives he set. I am really grateful for his input. Here he's speaking about the importance of building a solid bond and relationship with people.

I was very fortunate to meet Mark Wallage about 30 years ago. At that time, Bryan Holliday and I owned a fledgling audio-publishing company focusing on self-help titles, aimed mostly at schools, colleges, and public libraries. We'd both had prior experience with a publishing company producing careers guidance titles, in England, for the schools market.

Mark at that time was working for a New South Wales government department, providing vocational guidance. We commissioned him to produce a series of audio tapes explaining what it was like to be working in a range of different occupations. We were impressed with Mark's ability to write, cast, direct, and produce finished product ready for market. They sold well. And it was this all-round creative and communications ability that Mark brought to bear over many years, producing for us numerous video programs and hundreds of live ceremonial, recognition, and training events for corporations, government agencies, and associations. In every case, Mark took a brief, usually enhanced it, proposed creative treatments, and delivered an end product to satisfy us as executive producers and our clients.

So how did we manage him? This really wasn't a problem. Despite many invitations to join us full-time, Mark always preferred to work freelance, giving him the freedom to accept other clients' work and access to production studios where much of his film work was shot and edited. He attended pitch meetings with us and progress meetings as the projects unfolded. At live events, he took on the role of producer and show caller... calling for unusual levels of confidence, nerve, and clarity under enormous pressure. No surprise that he was engaged as a Sports Event Producer by two Olympic Games and other international sporting events.

In a nutshell, we had total faith in Mark. He always came up with a creative idea, he always delivered the goods, and there was no need ever to change him. We had great respect for his creativity and he appreciated the idea of working through our conference and communications business with a wide range of blue-chip accounts. Many of these clients were senior doctors, scientists, and business leaders. Mark was able to understand their language and quickly gained their confidence. To all intents and purposes, Mark was part of our team, carrying a business card in our company name, though technically he freelanced. I can't think of any disagreements over the 30 years and now that I am semi-retired, I continue to keep in touch with him as he develops his own business, Concept Event Management Pty Ltd.

What stands out for me here is Ian's genuine respect for Mark. You don't build a relationship for 30 years without it. But building a relationship that lasts 30 years also requires a certain amount of creative freedom, autonomy, and guidance. Knowing Ian, it doesn't surprise me.

Long-term relationships with your freelancers are built on respect. They require creative freedom, autonomy, and guidance.

GIVE FREELANCERS OWNERSHIP

One of the most successful events I ever directed still holds the title of Australia's largest ever corporate event. It consisted of four shows with an audience of about four thousand people each time: a huge musical dance extravaganza specifically created for one client. The stage was three tiers high and we had over 120 performers including dancers, bands, roving street performers — the works. On top of that, we had a host of people supporting them: costume designers, stage managers, choreographers, make-up artists, musical directors, and the like. Plus all the technical support.

When you're working with that many people and a very intense project, getting the right mix of people and the best people is paramount. But then you need to trust them, let them do what you've contracted them to do, and find ways to gain their input and help them take ownership. Otherwise, you've got a bunch of people just doing what you tell them to do — when they're the experts.

For instance, my head choreographer and lead dancer were Kate Kermond and her husband, Wayne Scott Kermond (Peter Allen Moe award winner). Having worked with them many times, I knew the moment the brief came in that they were the two people I wanted to headed up the dance team.

When it came to casting the dancers, I believe I made a very smart move. I got them involved right from the start and asked them to take the lead on casting the dance captains and the dance ensemble.

That did two things. Firstly, it gave them ownership. Because they had a stake in who was to perform, it made them an integral part of the process, created commitment, and gave them an emotional stake in the show. Secondly, it gave us access to the very best people. I'm not a dancer and I would never pretend to know what to look for in a dancer, especially when it comes to the different roles, requirements, and types of dance. That's their expertise and so I needed to trust that, flatten the pyramid, and give them autonomy in that process.

Did we get the best dancers because of it? Yes, we did. We did, in terms of the best right dancers for us. Our team included some of the very best dancers in Australia and some not, but that didn't matter — as a team, they were the best we could ever have hoped for and they were perfect for creating the show we needed. We made sure they understood the concept of the show, why it existed, the reason behind any changes we made, the client's needs, any cultural differences, technical aspects of how everything would work, and anything we felt would help them feel part of the entire event. We also listened to their suggestions. And it was the same philosophy with everyone who worked with us as part of the team.

What that means is that on paper you can get the best people, you might even get the right people, but to get the best-right people takes more than just recruitment and casting. You need to make them feel part of the process and the outcome. You need to make sure you're all on the same page, working towards the same things, so they can take the reins and give that extra something that makes all the difference.

THE NUTSHELL

Pulling together the right team is vital when it comes to leading creative people. Remember that creatives love hanging out with other creatives. So you need to consider getting the right skills base as well as the right diversity, the right harmony, and the right mix of behaviours in your team.

So it's about looking for the right fit. The future of your creative health is on the line here: find the people you really want and who really want to be there, and recruit them the way you want. When working with freelancers, remember to treat them as part of the family, as if they are under your employment.

It's about getting the best-right people and, like casting a film, when everything and everyone aligns, it's powerful stuff.

It's about giving people ownership, which is exactly what we're going to talk about next.

07: Getting Ownership

When you're building a great creative company, you can do everything right when it comes to identifying and understanding creative people, leading the right way, hitting the right motivators, building great teams, and avoiding the creative killers and frustrations, but you'll still be a long way from bridging the creativity gap. You'll have a great team of creative people who will excel and give you way above adequate. You'll be outpacing your competition, driving real commercial value for you and your clients, and everything will start falling into place. But you still won't be running at 100%.

Once you get those things under control, the art then becomes knowing how to get your creative people to take ownership of their creativity and their ideas, of what they're doing and why they're doing it.

In other words, you need to start focusing on ways to get your people taking ownership.

OWNERSHIP NOT BUY-IN

You'll notice I say *ownership*, not *buy-in*. There's good reason for that: getting buy-in is much easier to do and doesn't necessarily mean your people will take ownership of things. It may sound pedantic, but it's an important distinction.

Henri Lipmanowitz described the difference between the two clearly and succinctly. He put it like this:

Ownership is when you own or share the ownership of an idea, a decision, or an action plan; it means that you have participated in its development, that you chose of your own accord to endorse it. It means that you understand it and believe in it. It means that you are both willing and ready to implement it.

Buy-in is the opposite: someone else or some group of people has done the development, the thinking, the cooking, and now they have to convince you to come along and implement their ideas/plans.

So it's ownership we're after. Let me explain why.

CARROTS, STICKS, AND THE EFFORTLESS LEAP

My wife works with horses. It's in her blood. For whatever reason, she was put on this planet to be with and work with horses. I don't know why, I just know it's true. We all have a certain something that works for us — that thing where we just know we're going with the grain. It's feels right; it's what our inner soul, inner purpose, or natural talent is. You look at my wife riding a horse and even if you know nothing about horses, you know: it's right, it fits, it's exactly what she's meant to be doing.

One day, having attended a training session, she was telling me that the best way to get a horse to do what you want it to do is to get the horse to *want* to do what you want it to do.

If you need to read that again, here it is. 'The best way to get a horse to do what you want it to do is to get the horse to want to do what you want it to do'.

Which is pretty obvious, but also pretty profound. It's the difference between getting *buy-in* and *ownership*.

You see, you can actually get a horse to do lots of things by getting its buy-in. For example, if you want the horse to jump a creek, you can give it a carrot or whack it with a stick. The horse will buy in to that: it will take part in the exercise, because it either wants the carrot or doesn't want a sore derrière. Of course, if you want the horse to keep jumping the creek, you're going to need a lot of carrots. As my wife pointed out, carrots don't actually work — after a while, the horse won't do anything without one. Sticks don't work either, because eventually the horse becomes immune to the whack. Sure, it might keep doing what you ask, but that's about it. It probably won't be very pleasant or graceful, and you're going to have to put a lot more effort in.

To get the very best out of your team, you need to find ways for them to take ownership

Surely a better alternative is finding a way to make the horse *want* to jump the creek — rather than making the poor equine beast jump it because it has to. That's where ownership comes in.

If you want an effortless leap, one that is graceful, exciting, exhilarating, and safe, then you want the horse to take a certain amount of ownership of the situation. You want it jumping the creek because it wants to, because it has a say in the matter. That's the wonderful moment when horse and rider are working together as one. It's telling the horse what needs to be done and letting the horse do it.

THE CREATIVE LEAP

Trying to get people to be creative and come up with ideas is exactly the same. You've got to find ways for them to take ownership if you want ideas and solutions that are gold, if you want them to take the creative leap, and if you want them to follow their ideas through with passion, heart, and soul.

Think about it: how many brainstorming sessions have you sat in which were completely ineffective because your team just weren't engaged? Sure, they may have *bought in* to the process, but they may have felt that they had no stake in the outcome, that it was beyond their control, or that they were just a part in the machine. They may even have come up with above adequate ideas and solutions, because they still participated. What they gave was good enough. But that's a very different thing to taking the creative leap and it's not running at 100%. *That* only comes with gumption, heart, fire, passion — in a word, ownership.

If you want commercially viable results, if you want to add real value for your clients and to your bottom line, then good enough doesn't cut it. Anyone can do good enough. It takes an extra something to take the creative leap and run at 100%. *That's* how you get the gold.

I have an absolute, undying belief that for creativity to really leap, and to get the very best out of your team, you need to find ways for them to take ownership. Otherwise, it's a complete waste of time.

This is why finding good creative people is not your problem. Good creative people can be found everywhere. The art is getting those people engaged and passionate about what they do and what you do. That way, they'll be able to run at 100% and come up with really astounding solutions.

And in my experience, coming up with ideas is never the problem either. The world is full of ideas. The art is getting your team fired up, so they push past the first rung or idea, past the second rung, to the top level of truly unique, truly useful, truly innovative solutions that rock and change the world.

The art is in ownership: getting your people engaged and fired up so they own those ideas. So they pursue, live, and breathe their creativity with passion and with every fibre of their being. When you do that, you'll see possibilities you never imagined.

STOP TRYING TO GET PEOPLE TO DO STUFF AND START GETTING THEM TO *WANT* TO DO STUFF

So the game is getting ownership, which is completely different to getting buy-in. You can engage people, but you can't force ownership on them. You need to find ways to allow that to happen.

We can try as much as possible to make someone do something, but unless they really *want* to, it isn't going to happen. We can dangle as many carrots as we want, but that simply doesn't work well. Figuring out how to get *buy-in* from your people is carrot-and-stick stuff. Figuring out how to help your people take *ownership* is leadership stuff.

Remember the film producer? They need to know how to get the best out of each individual if they are to produce the best film. If each individual takes ownership of their area, then the producer has a much better chance of the whole film set taking ownership. If one individual doesn't, then the whole dynamic of the team can break down. Each individual needs to be engrossed in the whole film as well as their part. They may not be able to take ownership of what the director is doing, but they need to have the big picture in mind and understand the importance that they play in its success. In a way, they need to take ownership of the entire film.

You need to find out how to get your people emotionally fired up, not just about their role but also with the entire team, the entire project, and the direction of the organisation. Not because they're forced to, but because they want to.

So how do you give people ownership? Yes, you need to know what motivates creative people, but motivation can be supplied with a carrot. You need to reach that extra level — and you do that by finding ways for your people to take *ownership*. Here are some pointers.

LET THERE BE OWNERSHIP

LET PEOPLE ENGAGE

Serving as creative director on many large public and corporate events, I learnt that it was vital to have a team around me who took ownership of the role and the production. Part of my role was to find ways to make that happen.

By letting them share and be part of the vision of the event, they were able to see the importance of their role in the overall success. That adds a whole new layer to the game, a new dimension of commitment and excitement. It gives them the chance to be part of something bigger than themselves.

On an event I worked on in Singapore a few years back, I remember the moment our set designer saw his creation come to life. For months, we'd been working from a production office, and creating the set for the show was an integral part. It needed to have the right feel, the right look, complement the performance, be practical, and it needed to work for the show, not against it. Pete took amazing ownership of that. He was involved from the start, added great insights, and became a major part of the entire team. He understood everything else that was happening, how it affected him, and how he affected it.

He was so attached to it all that on the day the set was built at the venue, I remember the emotion he showed on seeing his baby come to life. It was the birth of something very real and close to his heart. It moved him, because it was part of him and he was part of it.

The point is, technically speaking, he could have just done his job at the start. And in theory, we didn't have to fly him to Singapore. But each of those factors would have been a huge mistake. By getting him involved from the beginning and including him in the whole success of the event, he was truly engaged and took ownership. That meant we got amazing results and effort far beyond someone just going through the motions and doing their job.

Rather than figuring out how to engage people, maybe the answer lies in allowing people to engage themselves. When they do, they'll take ownership.

That can take courage from a leader, because it means handing over a certain amount of control. But remember: a leader's role should be to guide and direct, not micromanage.

There is, however, a potential pitfall here. It isn't all that hard to give permission for people to take ownership and to help them take it. But if that ownership is taken away again, that defeats the purpose. Imagine working on an idea and really taking ownership of it, only to have it snatched from you. You'd feel deflated and not totally valued. Let's be realistic: that happens.

There are times when a project needs to move onto the next stage and when you need people to take ownership only for a certain time. As the director of a film, once it goes to print, the marketing and publicity is quite often out of their hands. There's a point when the controls are handed over.

When that's the case, you need to set the rules up front and let people know when it will occur. Then everyone knows their role and at what stage of a project their involvement starts, ends, or changes.

EMOTIONS DRIVE US

As people, we're emotional creatures. It drives us in every way. Think about it: every memory you have carries with it some kind of emotional connection.

When I think about some of my favourite memories, there's always a feeling — happiness, joy, love, elation, or contentment — attached to it. The birth of my kids, buying a new motorbike (well, for me anyway), landing the ultimate contract: they all

I hear and I forget.
I see and I remember.
I do and I understand.

— CONFUCIUS

carry an emotion. When I look back at my career, the moments which stand out are connected to very real and meaningful emotions, such as pride, elation, fun, happiness, and a sense of achievement.

When you watch an amazing film, it's the emotion it evokes that draws you in. With a romance, it's the packet of tissues you've gone through. If it's a good blow-em-up, it's the adrenaline rush and nail-biting excitement. If it's a comedy, it's the feel-good belly laughs that get you. We love films because of the emotional release they give us.

Emotions do more than just affect us, though. A very good friend of mine is an acting tutor. She's worked with the best of them and one day, taking part in one of her classes, I learnt something truly empowering.

One of the best ways to get people emotionally connected to a project is to get their involvement early on.

We were talking about what motivates a character. Actors are always looking for their motivation. In a scene with more than one character, it usually comes down to what you want the other person to do — kiss you, fight you, forgive you, or believe you, whatever. Sandra spun that around by asking the simplest of questions: 'Are you affecting the other person?' That is fantastic: it's not about getting them to do stuff, it's about getting them to *want* to do stuff. Affecting the other person becomes an emotional issue. That's where you look for the emotional connection to the person and the activity.

For instance, if you want them to kiss you, you don't just ask for it. You say or do something which so affects them that they can't bear *not* to kiss you. You find an emotional connection. The great thing is that they want to kiss you, because they've taken ownership.

As human beings, we are not just influenced by our emotions. Our emotions drive us. Now, I'm no psychologist, but I do know that's true. Neurologically speaking, according to Richard Cytowic, decisions are made in our emotional core, not our logical core — whether we like it or not, all decisions are emotional. It's part of being human. If you're excited about that next holiday, you'll be online booking it, thinking about it, talking about it, and driving your friends mad about it. I also believe it's the emotional connection to things that allows us to take ownership. So you need to find the emotional connection that fires your team up so that they own their ideas, their projects, and their creativity.

INVOLVE PEOPLE EARLY AND OFTEN

One of the best ways to get people emotionally connected to a project is to get their involvement early on.

If you bring someone in halfway through the game, suck their expertise out, and then say, 'Thanks,' what you have is buy-in. But if you can bring people into the game as early as possible, include them in your vision, explain the reasons and meaning behind the vision, ask for their opinion and cherish their expertise, then you're well on the way to getting their ownership. Especially if you follow through, keep them involved, and keep asking for their input. Remember: creatives like to know they are contributing to something bigger than them. They want to feel a part of things.

Personally, I think it's a big mistake to bring people in only when you need them. If you want them to get revved up and go beyond the call of duty, they need to feel part of the whole thing.

So involve your people as early as possible. That doesn't mean they need to be 100% on call from the very start. Realistically, their input will vary, depending on the need at the time — but they still can and will want to be across things and contribute as needed.

BE OPEN AND DIRECT

Creatives don't like bullsh*#. (Mind you, who does?) Keeping the communication channels open is one of the best ways to help a creative person feel part of things. For a creative, there's nothing worse than being kept in the dark or on a need-to-know-only basis. That means you need to be direct (to let them know what's happening) and open (to listen to them in return). However, it doesn't mean be bombastic or authoritarian (that's the old blunderbuss method of communicating).

Chat's a good thing, but it gets distracting if it heads off into tangents that have no substance behind them. Creatives like to know what's required of them, so just let them know and don't confuse the issue with frivolous talk. Keep it down to earth, to the point, and keep them informed. Be direct.

Of course, all communication is a two-way thing. As we saw, *not listening* was high on the creative killers list. There are times when creative people feel they are bashing their heads against the proverbial wall when it comes to being heard.

Part of that is because the creative mind often runs at a different pace to yours. Creative people tend to like talking shop and meander off into different subjects, topics, and areas of interest. Remember: they love exploring. Part of it is because many creative people find it hard to articulate their thoughts clearly (especially if they're visual). Part of it is down to leaders and managers not listening to what is being said. Either way, the communication channel breaks down.

It's essential to be open enough to listen to what is actually being said and to take it on board. Even if their ideas never see the light of day, the fact that they were heard is important — and is crucial for developing ownership.

AUTONOMISE IT

Creatively, it's really hard to get things done if you can't make the decisions you need to make. There must be a degree of autonomy, where your people are empowered to make decisions and get on with their jobs.

Having a structure that's too vertical hinders things getting done and leads to lack of creative freedom. Your creative people know what they're doing (at least, they should, otherwise they shouldn't be there) so let them get on with it and do what they do. Yes, you need to be across things, guiding the direction, and stepping in when things get out of hand, but your creative people must have a certain amount of autonomy. Otherwise, they feel smothered and they can't use their expertise.

...stop trying to get people to be creative and start trying to get them to want to be creative.

Again, it's like being a Hollywood producer. Your role is to guide the production, find the money, make sure all the resources are in place, and pull together the very best team. But then the members of that team need to be given some freedom to do what they do best. They need to be empowered to make decisions about their part of the production. You won't see a producer telling the make-up or lighting crew how to do their work. If you did, all hell would break loose on the set. Film sets establish levels of command; if the producer has issues, then they go through those levels. That allows people the creative freedom to be self-governing, while the commercial outcome is still guided and controlled from the top. Ultimately, the buck still stops with the producer, but autonomy in their job empowers everyone to get on with their job.

Empowering people leads to ownership. If people have a say in the decisions that are made, especially at the level they play at, then they will take control of those decisions and stand by them.

THE NUTSHELL

Yes, getting the best from creativity in your business is about nurturing and tapping into the creative potential of your people, then steering and directing that to achieve the desired outcome. But to make it really successful, you also need to find ways for your creative people to take ownership of their creativity, their ideas,
and their work.

Carrots and sticks won't work — you need ownership for people to take the creative leap. You need to stop trying to *get* people to be creative and start trying to get them to *want* to be creative. You need to help them find the emotional connection with their work, involve them early and often, give them autonomy, and be open, direct, and clear about the task at hand.

When people take ownership, it's really hard to make them *stop* giving you extraordinary results.

o8: Creative Risk

Being creative is a risky business. Without doubt, egos are on the line and personalities at stake. Business likes progress and success, not failure, but trying new things means falling over every so often. Failure and making mistakes is part of creativity — and the biggest risk a business can take, with creativity, is being risk-averse.

#1 creative killer: risk aversion.

Believe it or not, one of the biggest frustrations creatives have is organisations being risk-averse and having low tolerance for failure. In our survey, risk aversion came up as the Number One killer of creativity by a long way. Having worked with creative people and creative businesses, this doesn't surprise me at all. We've all experienced being creatively strangled by others who simply aren't prepared to take a creative risk. It's suffocating — and it smacks of megalomania. It's the biggest creative killer of them all. To be creative and explore possibilities, you need to step out and take creative risks.

Part of the leader's task is to create a culture where taking creative risks is simply part of what you do — where, in fact, it's encouraged. Create a place where people feel safe to be creative and voice their ideas. Provide a creative environment where it's safe to explore possibilities and put ideas on the table without fear of ridicule. Give your people permission to take creative risks.

Give your people permission to take creative risks.

But before you do that, you need to understand the value that taking risks *and making mistakes* can add to your business.

MISTAKES ARE A GOLDMINE

Know this: mistakes are simply part of the process — if you're being creative, then you are going to make mistakes. You can't 'do' creativity without them. Often, the very process of making a mistake leads to a new discovery and even greater success. Mistakes also bring us new things. Slinkys were a mistake. Post-its were a mistake. Penicillin was a mistake. We *need* mistakes.

LIGHTBULBS: MISTAKES ARE PART OF THE PROCESS

Thomas Edison failed over one thousand times to invent the lightbulb — maybe more, depending on who you read. But he saw every failure as his learning what didn't work. Tricky to imagine life without the lightbulb. And consider Steve Jobs, from Apple — there's a man who's failed quite a bit. He dropped out of college, was fired from his own company, and many of his ideas never made good. Who remembers the 'Next Cube'? But thankfully, failure leads to success and Steve Jobs pressed on. Apple isn't just about iPhones and iPads; it's about changing how we experience and connect with the world. Thank goodness Steve Jobs didn't fear mistakes!

We all make mistakes. It's part of being human and it's certainly part of being creative. It doesn't matter who you are or what you do: everybody makes mistakes. But mistakes don't mean the end of the world or the end of your business. They mean you're trying new things and moving forward. I don't believe that anyone did anything great or worthwhile without tripping up. Mistakes aren't the end of the road; they can lead to greatness, opportunities, and ultimately success.

PERFUME: MISTAKES LEAD TO SUCCESS

In 1874, a young man called David McConnell had an idea. As a door-to-door book salesman, he wasn't having much luck. He'd give his spiel and the door would slam in his face. Now back in 1874, it was usually the lady of the house who answered doors — the man would be off shooting elephants or running a coal mine or some such. Young David decided to get creative and offer his potential customers an incentive. He approached an acquaintance who made perfumes and cosmetics, and purchased a stock of testers — small glass phials of perfume.

His idea was this. When the lady of the house answered the door, he'd offer them free perfume if they listened to his spiel and didn't slam the door in his face. Quite inventive and not a bad idea, apart from the fact that it didn't work. He gave away a heap of perfume, but didn't actually sell any books.

A great idea — which failed.

Luckily, the story doesn't end there. Undeterred, our young hero had another idea and took another risk. What if he sold perfume instead? I don't know if he gave away free books as an incentive, but I do know it worked. David McConnell discovered that his potential customers liked buying the perfume. He saw new potential in his idea, started selling other cosmetic products, and a few years later he started a company called Avon. David McConnell changed the world of direct selling.

Fortunately for millions of Avon ladies around the globe, David McConnell didn't fear failure.

SLINKYS: MISTAKES ARE NEW IDEAS

In 1943, a naval engineer called Richard James was working on a design to mount ship instruments with a spring-loaded base. He was experimenting with a number of different types of springs, but in the process the springs fell off the bench. One of them kept falling — stepping, almost — down various levels until it reached the floor.

The Slinky was born: a simple toy, a soft spring that walks down steps, which has delighted millions. From that mistake, Richard and his wife took a risk. They invested some time and money, and created the James Spring and Wire Company. Like Avon, the rest is history.

Often things that pop up unexpectedly are pure gems. Out of the blue comes what looks like a complete failure, but is in fact a gold mine — if we just recognise it, that is. If we're open enough to see it, not as an irreversible mistake, but as an opportunity and a gift.

The Slinky was one of those wonderful mistakes where from a mistake comes something magical. I can't help wonder how many slinkys slip through our fingers every day because we're not prepared to take a creative risk and to see failure as opportunity.

Another great example of this is the 3M Post-It Note —
a mistake that made good when inventor Art Fry accidentally
stumbled upon a new use for an adhesive. According to Xavier
Waterkeyn, in his book *Brilliant Ideas*, the story goes that Art
invented a semi-sticky glue which no-one could work out what
to do with. But rather than simply discard and throw it out,
'the company shelved the idea as a curiosity.' Some six years
later, Art was in church, attempting to mark his hymnal book
with bits of paper that kept falling out, and he remembered the
glue. The rest, of course, is history. It's become an amazing
success story — and the most amazing part is that 3M didn't
just discard the idea, but kept hold of it. In fact, they have a
policy called 'bootlegging', which allowed Art the time to work
on finding a commercial application for his unique glue.
In other words, they allowed him to play with the mistake
to see if anything could come from it.

HOW DO YOU REACT TO MISTAKES?

Somewhere in the world today, in some company, someone
got creative and had an idea. Whoever they are and whatever
the idea was, they flexed their creative muscles, took a creative
risk, and maybe even failed. If they failed, then one of two
things happened.

Either they were congratulated for their ingenuity, felt
encouraged to move on, and their creativity was given the
chance to evolve and develop into something wonderful.
That person's creativity was nurtured. Maybe the failed idea
will never get up, but the creative spirit of that person and
those around them will.

Alternately, their creative spirit was squashed and reined in —
and with it, the creative spirit of those around them. Ultimately,
the creative capital of the company was decreased.

Creative people understand the value of failure. Maybe not
commercially, but certainly creatively, because they know the
importance of experimenting, being curious, and trying new
things. It's this ability that allows them to find new possibilities
and discover new things. In fact, they'll go out of their way
sometimes just to try something and see what happens.

Business also needs to understand the value of failure and the commercial gain it can bring. It's important to understand creative risk, not be scared by it, not just tolerate it, but encourage it. Creatively and commercially, failure is an imperative skill.

Ask yourself: does your business have a tolerance for failure? Does it see failure as part of the process or as a major block? Do your people feel safe putting ideas on the table without fear of repercussion? Are your creative people seen as incompetent if they fail, or courageous?

We need to create environments where people feel comfortable taking creative risks, not inhibited, and where failure is seen simply as a step towards success — because that's where great ideas often come from.

GLEAN THE RICHES FROM MISTAKES

Think about all the great success in the world that has come from failure. Narrow that down to all the opportunities and success that have come about in your own life from mistakes. It's clear that failure has great value. Just think about it for a moment: how much money has been made from Avon, lightbulbs, or Post-It Notes?

Get curious about mistakes.

Many business leaders innately understand the importance of failure. Unfortunately, most businesses aren't good at tolerating it and don't allow their creative people to take creative risks.

In an interview on businessweek.com, Sunil Sinha of Tata Group (a large Indian conglomerate who, amongst other things, make the world's cheapest car) talked about the importance of 'failed innovation' — about being comfortable and open with failure. Tata Group works hard at fostering a culture of sharing stories of failure and learning from them. Our friends at Atlassian don't just understand failure — they're proud that they encourage a 'culture of failure'. According to Robyn Munro, 'We try to create an environment where it's okay to try something and fail.'

There lies the key. It's one thing to be okay about making mistakes and tolerate them; it's another to know how to benefit from them.

If you don't learn from mistakes, they aren't very useful. So building a culture that's okay with failure and learns from it is priceless. You also need to capture mistakes, so that their lessons, or their potential, don't get lost. Otherwise, mistakes aren't profitable. You need to get curious about mistakes, so you can learn from them and cash in on them. You also need to record mistakes. Jot down a note or have a wiki page for everyone to note stuff down. That way, it's never lost.

I reckon there are three responses to making mistakes. One is to get upset about them and try avoiding them — which, ironically, is a big mistake! The second is to accept it and say, 'Oh well, mistakes happen,' then move on and try again, which is far better. The third option is to get curious and ask, 'What's the lesson here?' or 'What's the opportunity?' That's a very different approach.

DON'T FEAR RISK

There are many reasons why people become risk-averse and here are four of them: fear of change, fear of ridicule, fear of pissing people off, and rewarding the average instead of the great.

1. FEAR OF CHANGE

Sometimes the best stuff is off the main road.

We know the normal tried-and-true road to success works, and deviating off-course is often seen as either unnecessary or risky. We don't want to disrupt the status quo. But guess what? In today's world, more than ever, maintaining the status quo could be the biggest risk you take. The world is changing: unless you change with it, the road you're on could end up at a ghost town with nobody left.

#5 creative killer: status quo.

In the country with my kids recently, we deviated off the main road. For miles, we saw nothing and no-one — and then, all of sudden, we hit pay dirt. Great views, sites of old ruined buildings, a beautiful campground, and a terrific time had by all. Sometimes the best stuff is off the main road.

A frequent appearance on the creative-killers list was the catch cry, 'That's not the way we do things around here!' If being creative is all about exploring new ground, then divorcing the

To live a creative life,
we must lose our fear
of being wrong.

—JOSEPH CHILTON PIERCE

status quo is essential. You can't create new stuff if you only want the old stuff; you can't implement new stuff if you're clinging onto the old stuff. Old ideas can evolve — but not if you want them to stay just the way they always have been. The mentality of *the-way-things-are* is completely counterproductive for creativity.

Try asking 'Why?' 'Why not?' or 'What if?' That feels safer for many than throwing away the entire 'way we do things'. By challenging it, you are recognising it and opening the door to moving on.

2. FEAR OF RIDICULE

We've all been there — sitting at a client briefing or a think tank, someone has a brainwave, and they voice it, only to be shot down in flames and told it simply won't work. What happens? That person's creativity is shut down. You're not getting another idea out of them. Worse still, everyone else in the group now shuts down, because they don't want to be next.

Creativity can be a very personal thing. As a result, we can become rather vulnerable. Luckily, many creative people have developed thick skin and don't pay too much attention to this sort of thing. But in their eyes, it usually lessens their opinion of the person who made the remark. Even if their creativity is unscathed, they're not going to give you their next idea.

#2 creative frustration: don't tolerate their mistakes.

Know this! If you're creative, you're going to make mistakes. If you're not making mistakes, you ain't doing nuffin. I once heard a speaker on innovation saying that only one in ten innovative ideas ever got up and running. That sounds about right — if anything, a little conservative. Mistakes come with the territory.

Personally, I have always thought it's a good rule not to on dump anyone's creativity. Even bad ideas can evolve into great ones. Creative people need to feel safe to throw an idea on the table without fear of ridicule.

3. FEAR OF PISSING PEOPLE OFF

People fear upsetting their superiors and their clients. This is true not just of leaders and managers, but of some creatives as well. The prospect of an unhappy client or an unhappy boss is often just too much to bear. Pushing the creative envelope and coming up with provocative, challenging ideas does risk upsetting people — especially people who cling to the status quo and to safe, adequate ideas. The fear of pissing people off can and does inhibit the creative process.

It's up to you to create a safe haven for your team to voice their ideas without any fear of upsetting someone. You need to be a good sounding board without passing judgment. At times, you also need to be a buffer between your creative people and your client in order to protect both of them.

4. REWARDING AVERAGE

Rewarding the average squashes any need to take creative risks. If you reward people for coming up with average ideas and average solutions, then being average is all you will get. It's easy to come up with safe, adequate ideas — *really* easy — but if you want to come up with the next iPod, you need to reward your people for going beyond average and being creatively extraordinary. For that to happen, you need to let them take creative risks and not be scared of failing.

Being creative is all about exploring new territories and going where no creative mind has gone before. That takes courage. Your creative people need to have courage — but so do you, to let them take creative risks, to be brave enough to stand by and watch when they fall.

Of course, sometimes the demands dictate average. Sheer time pressure or budgetary constraints can require compromise. That's a fact of life. None of us like it, but let's not encourage it or reward it.

Helicopters

Creatives need to be helicopters and their leaders need to build the heliports.

One of my favourite books is *The Art of Looking Sideways* by designer Alan Fletcher. It's a book of creative ponderings and observations and in it he draws an analogy with helicopters and vending machines.

The helicopters are those people who look at a project or problem from all different angles and perspectives. They hover high above the terrain to see everything in its entirety, to get the big picture. They then zoom in, getting nice and close to see all the detail. They fly around and see the terrain from as many different vantage points as possible. And because they see problems from so many perspectives, they can see endless possibilities.

Vending machines

Then you get the vending machines. These are the creatives (or creative companies) who have a range of standard solutions and ideas already in place. Clients put their money in the slot and out come the same old off-the-shelf solutions, wrapped up a little bit differently.

The problem is that many companies, in their quest to win over a client or get a project out quickly, settle for the vending machine approach. Yes, it delivers solutions and ideas — but only adequate ones, not the best ones, not the great ones.

As creative people and leaders of creative teams, we need to be helicopters. Being creative is about seeing the world from different perspectives and from fresh, unique angles. Be open to as many possibilities as you can: from possibilities come great ideas. If you limit the possibilities like a vending machine, you limit the value and quality of ideas.

To be truly creative is to be a helicopter

But there's something even more important. Without the right ground support, a brilliant creative will never get airborne. It's vital for leaders to hire, develop, and retain helicopters. Great leaders of creative people build heliports and maintain safe air space to work in. They know it's important because that's where the great ideas come from and that's what compounds their creative currency.

Being creative is all about exploring possibilities, finding new ways of doing things, and boldly going where no creative mind has gone before. You need to fly around to see those possibilities. It'll never happen if you're stuck on the ground being a vending machine. You need a culture that allows people the freedom to do just that, to explore possibilities and investigate alternatives. From possibilities come great ideas. Exploring is about finding ways to let your people be helicopters.

It's a great analogy. Thanks, Alan.

TOP DOWN OR BOTTOM UP?

If risk aversion is such a barrier to cashing in on the creative talents of your people, then you need to find ways of destroying that barrier.

Ideally, that needs to come from the top and filter down through the organisation. Your creative people need to know the rules of the game, that it's safe to take creative risks, and that they can push the boundaries. They love that. And it's difficult to get creative when everything your leadership stands for is going against you. So somehow, someone at the top needs to give *permission* for creative risk-taking. If it comes from the top, your creatives will play hard, because they know they have permission to do so.

But we don't live in a utopian world and many times that simply isn't the case.

Alternatively, you can play bottom-up and give your team permission to take creative risks and make mistakes on a local or micro level. By that, I mean on a team level or project level and buffer them from the top end of town. If it's successful, then like ripples in a pond the whole failure culture can expand sideways and upwards. In other words, take matters into your own hands. This way is a lot tougher and it comes with other ramifications if it backfires — but it can be done.

This is where you, as a leader, need to become a diplomat. I'm not saying you should go against company policy or values — but if you can, give your team permission to take creative risks, then assess and evaluate the work before it goes up the line. If the risk-friendly culture isn't coming from the top, this a good step forward.

Putting my creative hat on, I don't enjoy working for risk-averse clients. It restricts me creatively and it simply isn't enjoyable. As a creative, I wouldn't enjoy working for a risk-averse company either. I wouldn't hang around — I'd go find a company more in tune with the creative process.

At the end of the day, if a risk-averse culture constrains their creativity, your creatives will just get frustrated and leave. They'll just go work somewhere else.

THE NUTSHELL

Risk aversion is Number One on the list of creative killers. It stifles the creative flow and leads to adequate ideas, not world-changing ones. If you're being creative, you will make mistakes and you will experience failure. Accept that as a part of creative life, deal with it, and use it to your advantage.

Creative risk is simply part of the deal and it's madness to want creative solutions to things while playing it safe. They just don't go together. So you need to understand that by nature your creative people will experiment and do things that drive you mad, cause errors, and sometimes ruin things. They will make mistakes. If they aren't doing that, then you've got the wrong creative people in your team. But guess what? Because of that, they will also break new ground and discover amazing solutions and ideas which will allow you to outpace your competition so much more.

You need to give them permission to take creative risks, provide an environment and culture where it's safe to make mistakes, and protect your team from those who are risk-averse.

Like the gold rush days, 'There's money in them thar mistakes!' And remember: to get a ounce of gold, you need to dig through tons of mud and dirt.

09: **The Freedom of Structure**

One of the great ironies of creativity is this: in order to have the creative freedom you need, you also need to have a creative structure in place. Creativity loves structure, it thrives on it, but get it wrong and you'll either restrict it or have it meander and wander about without direction. So you need to have the right creative process, one that knows when to turn the creative controls on and off.

There is definitely an art in having the right process. In the introduction, we spoke about three rings: leadership, culture, and process. Process deserves a book all its own, which is why it gets one in this series: *Shooting Ducks*. For now, let's take some time to talk about the right creative process from the leader's point of view.

MANAGING THE INTANGIBLE BEAST

Let's revisit the intangible beast. We talked about how businesses wants to make the beast tangible and give it certainty, so they wrestle it into a cage and say 'Look! We have Creativity! And we can control it!'

Now once organisations trap the beast, they do one of two things. Either they fail to put a process in place to harness the beast's potential, or they put one in place that is so rigid it harms the beast.

This is because business likes certainty and is baffled by creativity. In the quest to make creativity work, business often implements rigid, cookie-cutter processes that only inhibit creative flow. Alternately, in the quest to be more creative, without fully understanding creativity, it takes away all the controls. Either way, you end up with inefficient and ineffective creative outcomes.

THE INTANGIBLE BEAST NEEDS STRUCTURE

The lack of a process comes from not knowing what to do with the beast once it's caged. Because it's not concrete or black and white, it appears to be a difficult thing to manage. Only 31% of our survey's participants said they had a creative process in place to harness and direct creativity.

#2 creative killer: lack of structure (or the wrong structure).

Creative people like structure and like to know the rules of the game. It's one of the great paradoxes. Structure — processes, guidelines, and parameters — allows creative people to know what's expected of them and what's not; it gives them direction and purpose. Without structure, it's difficult to know what to do next. You can still get stuff done, but it tends to have little purpose or meaning.

Creatives like structure, because it helps them get things done. But getting the structure wrong — too constrictive or too unstructured — only inhibits the creative flow and ultimately the outcome. So yes, creatives love having clear direction, knowing what the rules of the game are, and what boundaries to play within. But they also need the freedom to figure out how to get it done.

Creative people like structure and like to know the rules of the game.

THE INTANGIBLE BEAST NEEDS FREEDOM

The reverse problem is when businesses employs rigid systems to control the beast and put it to work. They implement systemic, step-by-step processes and paint-by-number procedures. It all becomes very formulaic, with what amounts to a 'Do **A** then **B** then **C**' protocol. By introducing these rigid controls, they are in fact restricting how creative you can be.

Yes, creativity needs structure and it needs process. But if that structure and process is too rigid and controlling, you get strangled creativity. If you lock the beast in a cage, poke it with a stick, and force it to breath fire, all you'll do is make it angry.

We will either find a way,
or make one.

—HANNIBAL

Ultimately, by constraining it, you'll kill the beast. The beast needs to be let out of the cage. It should never be there in the first place. It needs to roam free, to play, to explore, and do whatever it is the beast does.

Of course, if the beast is allowed to go absolutely rampant and do as it pleases, without any control or guidance at all, then it can become completely unmanageable and quite scary. That's probably why most people stick the beast in the cage in the first place. They're scared to let it loose in case it causes damage or they lose control of it. This seems to be a tricky conundrum — but it doesn't have to be that way, nor should it be. There is a happy medium.

THE INTANGIBLE BEAST NEEDS A LEAD ROPE

You need to place the beast on a lead rope. Not a short one — a long one, so it can wander about, explore, do its thing, be itself. Because you direct the lead rope, you can steer and guide the beast as needed. It will then be happy, content, *and* productive.

Don't kill the beast. You need it and it needs you.

The beast is happiest and most productive when it has clear direction, knows that it serves a purpose and a place in the world, and can still be itself. If it's left to go rampant, without any clear purpose, it loses its edge. The best thing you can do is to have a loose-tight relationship with it.

In other words, to manage the creative process, you need to know when to turn the creative controls on and off, rather than micromanage and cage it.

Don't kill the beast. You need it and it needs you.

Part of the leader's job is to be very clear: not just on your vision, but also in setting and communicating those guidelines and parameters. At the same time, you need to be brave enough and wise enough to let your creative teams do what they do best without getting in the way — just steering them occasionally when they get off-track.

You need a process that knows when to turn on and off the creative controls and directs creativity to your desired outcomes. One of the great ironies is that creativity thrives on structure, but the structure must also allow creative freedom.

You need a process that allows your creative people to explore and play, to think intangibly in order to find possibilities — but which then funnels and steers those possibilities towards tangible ideas and solutions. You need to create a tight-loose-tight process:

- tight — establish clear direction and very clear objectives and boundaries

- loose — let the creative beast play and explore within those boundaries

- tight — once creative possibilities have been explored, start analysing and evaluating them

In that sense, creativity is like a big funnel. Here's how it works.

THE FUNNEL

Just before you enter the funnel, you are in the tight phase, because this is where you need to establish clear direction, objectives, and boundaries — in other words, have a very clear and purposeful brief.

Then the top part of the funnel is where you explore possibilities — the helicopter phase. This is the loose phase, because this is where you let the intangible beast play; this is where creativity does its thing.

As you move down the funnel, the possibilities, ideas, and concepts you've discovered are filtered according to their value and usefulness. This evaluation, or filtering, is another tight phase.

Finally, the best outcome emerges from the bottom of the funnel.

ENTERING THE FUNNEL: BRIEFS

When you enter the funnel, you must be clear about what you're trying to achieve and what the task at hand really is — in other words, what you want to come out the funnel at the other end. That sets your direction and gives you a clear purpose. You must also establish the parameters and boundaries you need to work within, because they too will guide you.

Be clear

Creativity works best with clear direction. It's difficult to come up with creative solutions if you're not even sure what the problem is. One way to stop creativity in its tracks is to be uncertain and unclear about what it is you're aiming to achieve.

#7 creative killer: unclear goals and poor briefs.

You may think you have a simple objective or brief — but because everyone has different points of view, others may interpret the objective differently. That means you're working towards different things. What's more, briefs and objectives often aren't conveyed simply and concisely in the first place. If you want to annoy a creative person, just give them a whaffly, long-winded, or unclear brief. That serves no-one, plus it leaves the brief open to interpretation.

Be pedantic about clarifying your goals or brief. Make them as concise and as clear as possible. Make sure they're easy to articulate and that everyone understands the true heart of the matter. Do this throughout the entire line, from the client to the creative and from the creative to the client.

Keep it varied

If you keep giving your creatives the same types of brief from the same clients, in the same capacity, just because they did a good job last time, they'll get bored and switch off. You might get results, but the quality and inspired nature of those results diminish.

#6 creative frustration: same, same, same.

Creative people love variety. They're curious by nature. That's what creativity is all about — trying new things, exploring new territories. It's what keeps creative people fresh and inspired. It allows people to discover new things and push the boundaries. Remember the think-a-vator? They might do a great job, but too long in that quadrant and they'll lose interest.

Creative people have a low boredom threshold. That's a good thing and you should be delighted about it: it keeps them curious. It explains why creative people often appear to be all over the place, doing a myriad of different things, and being quite erratic. But for them, it's perfectly normal; it's part of the process of keeping things fresh. This is one of the reasons I like the analogy with herding monkeys.

Whatever you do, mix it up, challenge them, and keep things interesting.

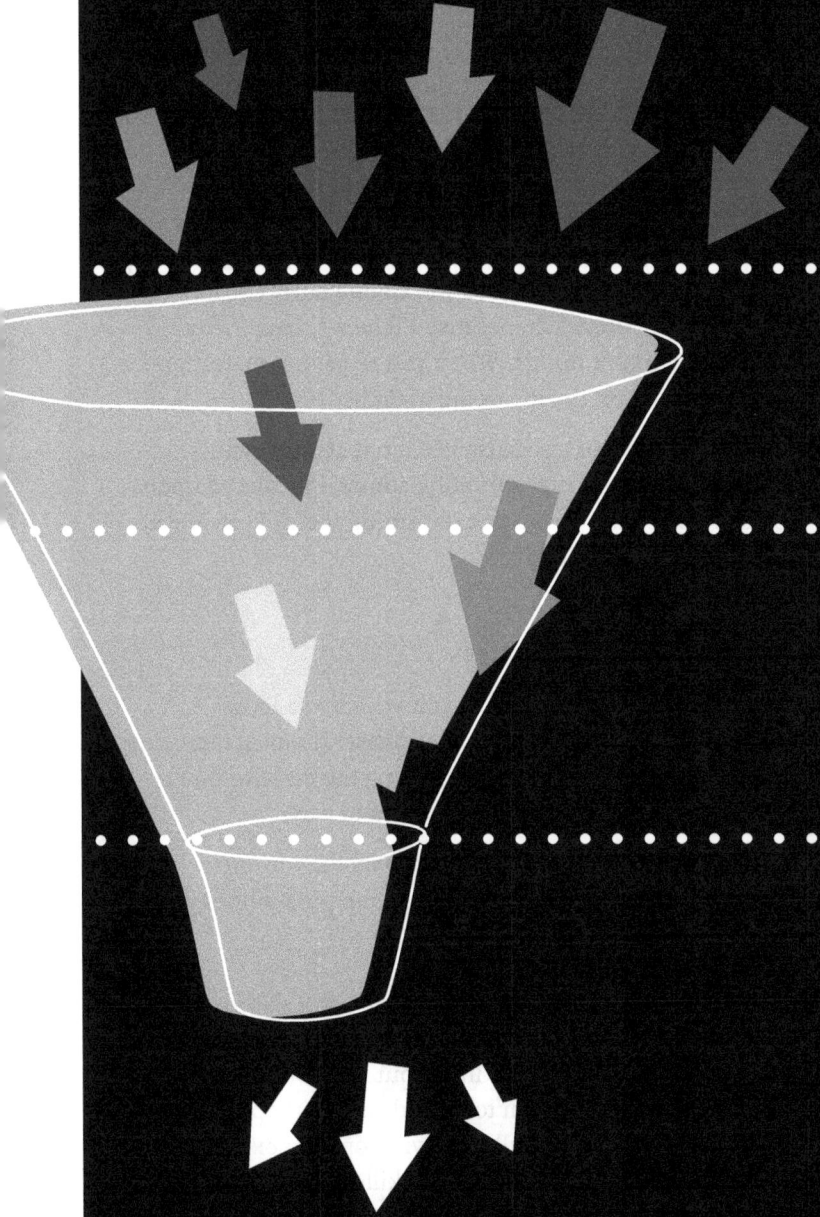

THE FUNNEL

Briefs

Helicopter
thinking

The filter

Be realistic: good, fast, cheap

I received this gem from Scott Crider. I love it, because it's not only true but also incredibly useful. Here's what he said:

'I've often said to clients and employers, when appropriate: "Good, fast, cheap. Pick any two."'

This simple concept drives home the root of the creative process for me. You can have good work done fast — but it won't be cheap, because I'll have to work some nights and weekends, and possibly bring in some freelancers to get it done for you. You can have it fast and cheap — but it's not going to be any good. You can even have good work done fairly cheaply — but it won't be done fast, because I'll be working it around other more urgent things. When you're paying mates-rates, your work isn't on the top of the to-do list.

Scott's quote is great, because it's about dealing with, accepting, and working within the constraints placed upon you and your team — but not rewarding them. Protect your team from unrealistic briefs.

INSIDE THE FUNNEL: STAY OPEN

Once you're inside the funnel, you switch to a loose relationship. This is the helicopter phase: it's all about being open to possibilities and not inhibiting the creative flow. This is where the intangible beast gets to play.

#6 creative killer: my ideas are better than yours.

Remember — the filter is at the *bottom* of the funnel. *That* is where you evaluate and judge the possibilities you've discovered.

Stay open

One of the creative killers surprised me, at first: 'My ideas are better than yours.' But thinking about it, I don't know why. Everyone should stay open to new ideas... perhaps it's easy to assume that they should all be staying open to *our* great ideas! Everyone includes us. This creative killer is about hanging onto what you think the best idea is, and not being willing to let go and see things from other points of view.

It's not just leaders who do this: so do clients and so do creatives (although they're less prone to this disease). You need to recognise when this is happening and help the process move on. Your ideas, or the ideas of one of your team, might be better — but that doesn't mean you should limit your creative options and stop listening to others.

Because ideas are personal, we tend to hang on to them. Rather than throwing ideas away, just park them for a while. That way you're not totally discarding anything at this point.

This is closely linked to the issue of not listening. Not listening is a three-pronged issue — a trident, if you like. The first two prongs are internal communication: managers and leaders not listening to their creative people, and creative people not listening to the leaders. It's part of the creativity gap. Each side closes themselves to the other side's views, or clings on bombastically to what they think is right. But we're all on the same team.

#4 creative killer: not listening.

The third prong is just as pointy — external communication. As Maurice Skivington of PWC Consulting (Director, Strategic Services) eloquently stated, it's 'holding your hands over your ears and going "Naa... naa... naa..." when your clients and customers are talking.'

Not listening is dangerous and it's damaging. We all know the power of shutting up, but it isn't always easy to do. Especially when you have a million ideas to talk about.

Listening goes beyond just hearing: it's about understanding each other, knowing each other's needs, listening to the real heart of the matter, and being open. Just sit and listen. Ask questions and aim at getting the focus off you and onto the other party. Try a 60% rule: for 60% of the discussion, you just listen and don't talk.

Just sit and listen.

Maybe it's worth having a game plan prior to meeting with a client or a stakeholder, and agreeing to a listen-talk ratio. If you have creatives in your meeting with a client, know this: they will most likely want to talk about their ideas. So tell them that they will get a chance and to wait until you throw it to them. It's all in planning and strategising the meeting.

Flexible time

Another aspect of freedom and the loose relationship is time.

#3 creative killer: time.

Let's face it: the creative process doesn't work 9 to 5. But too often, creatives are locked into 9 to 5, given unrealistic deadlines, and forced to be creative within office hours. Sorry, but it doesn't always work that way. The creative process needs time to do its thing. And leaders need to harness its potential by letting their creative people be flexible with time.

Am I saying to let your creative people come and go as they please? No — but would that be so bad? Creative people need a certain freedom of time to tap into their genius. They need to ponder, investigate alternatives, sit and think, sit and not think, or wander about to find an answer. It's how the creative process works. You need some flexibility to harness time to your creative advantage.

Time is a crucial factor in creating the right creative environment, which is why we'll revisit it in *Creating Zoos*. For now, understand that the creative process and your creative people need time to do their thing. So give your creative people some flexibility with time. Remember: creative people like boundaries, but within those boundaries they also require freedom. Give them freedom and you will be by far the net winner.

LEAVING THE FUNNEL: THE FILTER

Finally, out the end of the funnel come a number of workable ideas which have evolved from the possibilities you saw and which are in line with your objectives and your purpose.

Having a long list of possibilities is one thing, but unless those possibilities measure up to your purpose and are relevant, then they're not very helpful. You need to hone them down to a short-list of workable ideas. In other words, you need to *filter* your ideas, to ascertain which ones are worth taking forward.

You do need to analyse and evaluate the possibilities you've discovered and the ideas you've had — but be warned: the biggest mistake people make is evaluating ideas too early in the process. If you evaluate or judge them too soon, they'll never get a chance to breathe life or evolve. The mistake most people make is putting the filter at the top of the funnel. That's why you need to let your creative people play in the 'helicopter phase' — so they can explore and discover possibilities without fear of being judged or analysed. Remember: your clear objectives and parameters will guide them.

Great ideas come from seeking and being open to possibilities. The funnel allows that to occur by guiding the process and still letting your people's creativity do its thing.

The biggest mistake people make is evaluating ideas too early in the process.

THE NUTSHELL

The great irony of creativity is that for it to thrive, it needs structure — but if that structure is too restrictive or too open, then it's either suffocating or directionless.

The intangible beast needs a lead rope, so you can guide it and direct it, but still let it play. If you have it on a short lead, it will only be stifled. Let it loose enough so you get the best from it.

Being creative is like a funnel: you need to have tight controls going in, loosen them up at the top of the funnel, and then tighten them again at the bottom. That way, the intangible beast gets to play and you get to direct it. In other words, you need to know when to turn on and turn off the creative controls.

When you get it right, it's worth celebrating — which is where we are heading to next.

10: Let's Crack Open the Bubbly and Celebrate

Imagine this.

You've just spent six months working on a major project. It could be anything — you decide. A new software application, a marketing campaign, a fashion range, a variation of an exciting product line, it doesn't matter, as long as it's close to your heart and experience.

During those six months, you've given it your all. Every moment, every second, has been dedicated to making it happen. You've pulled together a great team of creative people who have also worked just as hard. Not only did they do a great job, but they took ownership of the project and gave you their all, because making this project happen was important to them, as well.

After all the usual ups and downs, unseen obstacles, moments of sheer joy and sheer panic, the project is competed and hailed a raging success. Its execution is deemed brilliant, its results are way above expectations, and everyone on the team has reason to be proud.

Well done.

Now that this one is put to bed, the appropriate people in marketing, sales, or whatever take over, and the project is no longer your concern. You've done your part and it's in the hands of the next crusaders. But you're not dormant long, because the next big project comes along. It's just as big and just as important. So you reset the team and maybe recast it slightly to suit the new project. You have a two-week break and send the team off for down-time, to re-energise, and then you all begin the next gig.

But something weird happens. When you start the new project, the team seems flat. They're not as well bonded as before, not as enthused, not as motivated. It's hard to get their ownership this time around. Even after a break, even with an influx of new people, something just isn't clicking.

Something is missing. What's missing is the *celebration*.

WHY CELEBRATE?

After you've focused on and dedicated yourself to one thing for any length of time, then, no matter how successful it is, you need to celebrate the effort, trials, and tribulations when it ends.

#10 creative motivator: reward.

When Walt Disney embarked on the world's first full-length feature cartoon, many of his critics thought he'd overstepped the mark. It had never been done. Until then, cartoons were shorts, usually played as previews to the real stuff. Why would you pay to see a full-length 90-minute *cartoon* when you could pay the same money and see a full-length film with real actors? Madness!

But Disney, as always, saw the potential and went forward with his project. He knew getting it right would take a massive effort, making sure that every single frame was drawn the best it could be and that the film lived up to the highest quality Disney demanded. No doubt it was a tumultuous task, into which his cast and crew threw themselves. After all, it's one of his landmark films and a triumph of animation.

But Disney didn't just inspire and lead his people to make a great film. He also knew the importance of letting his team celebrate their effort, bask in each other's glory, appreciate their success, and let off some steam. In his book *Disney's World*, Leonard Mosley talks of how Disney's team celebrated by having an after-party once the film was released.

I don't know if that's where the after-party started, but I do know they are more than just an excuse to open the bubbly. They are a necessary part of the creative process. They allow your creative people to celebrate their hard work and their talents.

As a leader of creative people, you need to understand the importance of celebrating the end of a project — with genuine thanks, not a token gesture. Celebrating is more than having a good time and it's more than just bonding. It says, 'This chapter has finished,' so that the next one can start cleanly, without shadows or overtones from what went previously. It gives closure and resets the creative switch. It reinforces a sense of community and shows appreciation. It's morale-boosting, motivating, and uplifting.

So you need to help your creative team get a sense of closure, of accomplishment, and of a job well done.

CELEBRATING CREATES CLOSURE

It's crucial to celebrate successes, especially creative ones.

It's crucial to celebrate successes, especially creative ones. Cracking open the bubbly (even figuratively) and taking the time to pat yourself and your team on the back is like giving closure to a major part of your life so you can move on. Otherwise, you'll feel as if you've left it open-ended. You'll feel like you never really completed it. Part of the missing *something* is the closure you and your people need: the sense of completion.

But there are other payoffs as well. For some, it's like hitting the reset button: their creative system gets to shut down for a moment and then reboot, fresh and ready to go. For others, it's an adrenaline rush, which then carries them forward to the next great thing.

CELEBRATING ROOTS COMMUNITY

#2 creative motivator: recognition.

Remember: creatives love being part of a community and of something larger than themselves. Celebrating helps cement that. It's not just about hanging out with your peers and patting each other on the back, it's about a genuine sense of achieving great things as a group, of contributing to and of celebrating the creativity of others as well as yourself.

If creatives are moving on to new things and new teams, they also need to feel they can leave one community and be accepted into another. The last thing you or they want is to be hanging onto the last project and the people in it.

That doesn't mean they must walk away completely. Of course not: it's more of a ritual, where the team ceremonially celebrate their achievements and are officially accepted back into the greater tribe. Otherwise, there's a chance of people harking back to their shared triumph and then you get a 'when-we' effect — which is exclusive of everyone else.

At times, it's wise to invite *everyone* to the party, so you can help the others share in the success and celebration, and help the team dissolve back into the group. It may also be wise to display the finished project, ideas, or progress in some way — as a slide show, posters, models, or whatever's appropriate.

CELEBRATING REFILLS THE RESERVOIR

But it's not just at the end of the project that you should celebrate.

Creative energy is like a huge reservoir and as time goes on, there is evaporation and unexplained drainage. If you don't take care of it, it will eventually run dry. Enormous effort goes into a creative project (or any project for that matter) and at times you need to refill the reservoir. It can be a huge mistake to wait until the end.

In 2006, when I was contracted to direct a major corporate show in Singapore, we had a large cast of local performers and spent many weeks putting them through their paces, learning and rehearsing tightly choreographed routines.

About halfway through, we had a party — nothing big, just a get-together to let off steam and have a bit of fun. The result was a group of people who knew each other better, a sense of camaraderie, and greater trust. For me, it was a great leveller, allowing us all to be equal parts in a massive project.

Celebrating should happen when the time is right. Maybe it's when you and your team hit certain milestones on a project's journey. Maybe it's to celebrate a fresh, new idea that came out of nowhere. Maybe it's just to celebrate a creative notion or achievement one of the team has had.

But here's the important thing. It needs to be special. I'm not talking the standard Friday-night drinks here. Remember the carrots and sticks in chapter 7? Friday-night drinks can become carrots — and after a while, if you don't provide them, people get disgruntled. So when you celebrate, whenever that is, make sure it's genuine and heartfelt.

For creative people, finishing a project, contract, or creation can be a let-down. They've invested their creative and emotional energy into creating and when it's all over, there's often a void. One moment, it's all exhilaration and excitement, and then suddenly — it's all over. But the creative momentum doesn't stop; it just seems to hang around with nothing to latch onto. In some ways, it's like losing a lover.

A good friend of mine in musical theatre tells me that when he gets home from a show, it takes him a few hours to 'come down' before he can go to bed. When the show finishes, the adrenaline and rush from performing doesn't. It lingers and takes a while to dissipate. My editor, Megan Kerr, mentioned to me when we were chatting about this chapter that she always feels completely flat after finishing a novel.

Sometimes, just a simple word of thanks or recognising a spark of ingenuity is enough.

At Absurd, we made sure we hung out with the cast after an event. We chatted about the world, the next gig, and the new things the performers were working on. It helped cure the flatness of finishing a gig.

Flatness doesn't only come at the end of a project — it can also come at the end of a milestone or segment. As a leader, if you can recognise it, you can help alleviate it. Get creative with the solution, because there are many alternatives and it depends on the individual. Here are some starters...

- grab a coffee with them and chat about their thoughts and feeling towards whatever it is they have just completed

- keep their energy going with a slightly lesser task — that works a bit like a warm-down when you go to the gym

- send them out to an art gallery, beach, or whatever turns them on

- get them to help someone else

- or simply give them a day off

It's kind of fun
to do the impossible.

—WALT DISNEY

IT'S NOT JUST ABOUT CHAMPAGNE AND CAVIAR

Celebrating moments of creativity can be accomplished in a myriad of ways. It doesn't always have to be a huge after-party or a bottle of champagne.

Sometimes, just a simple word of thanks or recognising a spark of ingenuity is enough. Maybe it's a phone call after someone in your team went the extra mile creatively, when they didn't just push the envelope but tore right through it. It's one thing to appreciate someone's efforts and contribution, but another to actually tell them. That goes a long way.

Perhaps it's hiring the director's suite at the local cinema complex and having an exclusive viewing for the team of a latest release. We once took our team out for a wine-tasting day, jumping on an old DC3 propeller driver plane, and having cars drive us from vineyard to vineyard. One of my clients allows their creatives to choose a show, dinner, or anything that takes their fancy, up to a certain dollar value. It's not just about parties.

THE NUTSHELL

It's funny, but in our need to get stuff done, make our mark on the world, and drive creative value for our businesses, we often forget to have fun and celebrate along the way. Splurging and taking time out can at times seem frivolous and wasteful. After all, there are more important things to address — or are there?

Don't look on celebrating your creative achievements as a nicety or a luxury. It's a very smart strategy. It gives closure to projects, so your creatives are free to move on. It roots the community — and reroots your team within it. It refills the reservoir during a project or simply when it gets low. It helps cure any flatness from using loads of creativity.

But more than that, it helps creatives feel good about who they are and what they do. It gives them recognition and gratitude, and that in turn empowers them for greater things down the track.

Celebrating is an important skill in maintaining the health and vitality of a creative team. It inspires them.

11: The Quest

Let's finish by getting to the heart of the *creativity* matter, to what's really important. If we are to bring creativity to life in a business, so that it adds value and gets results, then we need to become great leaders of creative people. And to be great leaders of creative people, we need to inspire the creativity of others.

THE INVISIBLE POWER OF INFLUENCE

I remember rocking up to my dad's office as a young kid during school holidays and asking to see his films. He didn't work in the film business; he was in advertising. More specifically, he was the advertising director of Philips. His secretary (I don't think they had executive assistants back then) would amuse me by setting up a 16mm projector in a spare room and bringing out a pile of Dad's advertisements. I would sit there for hours, just watching the ads and promo reels, playing them again and again and again. I used to love the sound the film made when it was running through the sprockets, seeing the light glow in the projector and how the dust would flitter and play in its beam. Sometimes, just for kicks, I would play the films backwards. Very cool. My dad never said no to me watching his films. He was never too busy to bring a projector home to set up in the living room.

A few years later, when I was a teenager, he set up a meeting with a family friend who was a film producer, to chat with me about a career in the film business. That led to me getting work experience on a 70s soap opera, *The Young Doctors,* doing stand-by props — which in turn led to working on a film, *Hoodwinked* (which I'd actually forgotten about until now).

Around the same time, my mother owned an art gallery, so much of my teenage years was surrounded by people who appreciated creativity and the arts. People who also managed to make a living, and some of them very good livings, from their creativity. (At 80, my mother still painted.)

In contrast, during my final year of school, all I wanted to do was to work in the entertainment industry. I didn't know exactly what that meant (after all, it's a big industry), but somehow I knew that I wanted to entertain people. For a young lad of 17, that was probably all the direction I needed. The day I left school, a teacher asked what me what I was going to do (and yes, I do remember her name) and I said, 'I'm going to entertain people.' 'Oh... that's nice,' she said. At the time, I took it to heart: to me, that response was condescending and I believed for a long while that I possibly wasn't cut out for the creative world. Luckily, I had others around me with more faith, and eventually I listened to them and to whatever it was that drove me.

I am incredibly grateful that people who were supportive and open to creative endeavours surrounded me in my youth. People who didn't judge, mock, or try to interfere, but instead mentored, guided, and led by example. Just being who they were and doing what they did was an enormous influence.

There lies a great lesson. I learnt at a very early age, without even knowing it, that we each hold an immense power of influence over other people and that we can either draw the very best out of them or shut them down. We can inspire people to be their best or we can point them to mediocrity — without even knowing we're doing it.

A great leader of creative people knows that the first choice is a nobler one. Inspiring people to be their creative best is a much better choice.

SO HERE'S MY QUEST

I want to change the creative landscape of the world.

That's it. And I would love you to join me, because I can't do it alone.

It sounds big — but it's actually not that difficult. And it isn't difficult for a very simple reason. If each of us can inspire just one other person to be more creative, think more creatively, and act more creatively, and if each of us can just support, nurture, and encourage just one other person to tap into their creativity without fear of failure or ridicule, but instead with confidence and a sense of discovery and curiosity, then we will have already succeeded.

Maybe in a small way at first, but like the ripples in a pond that grow and gain momentum as they move out, these creative ripples will begin growing and gaining momentum as well. And if we can inspire many people to be more creative, the momentum only gets greater.

Change the creative landscape of the world.

Just imagine it: imagine the difference that would make, not just to individuals, communities, and economies, but to your business.

Imagine if we encouraged people to take creative risks, instead of hanging onto the status quo. Imagine if we gave our people permission to throw possibilities and ideas around as if there were an infinite supply. Imagine if we created an environment where being creative was not just something you do when you need to, but something you do every day, because it's part of your business's DNA. Imagine if your people felt inspired and encouraged to be more creative.

I love creativity and all things and people creative. I love seeing people tap into their creative side, using creative thinking to find practical business ideas and strategies, and I love helping people draw their creative side out of themselves.

This book began by saying that the challenge facing business with creativity is in knowing how to lead your creative people, how to harness their genius, and how to direct it towards viable business outcomes. And in our quest to be great leaders of creative people, we need to become great at inspiring the creativity of others. I don't just 'buy in' to that: I take complete ownership of it.

Because when that happens, not only will the creative capital of your business go through the roof, but together we really will have changed the creative landscape of the world.

And that is very, very sexy.

Books

Here's a list of some of my favourite books on creativity and on leading and inspiring creativity. This is not a bibliography but a reading list of some of my favourite books on the subject, and one that is by no means complete. In no particular order...

The Art of Looking Sideways — Alan Fletcher.
Phaidon Press, 2001.

If everything in my library but this book was stolen, I would be okay. I love this book. It's the ponderings of designer Alan Fletcher, full of gems and wonderful insights. It's a book not to read but to ponder your way through.

The Disney Way — Bill Capodagli and Lynn Jackson.
McGraw Hill, 1999.

A wonderful walk through the 'how they do things' of Disney, with some fabulous ideas and inspirations.

The Flight of the Creative Class — Richard Florida.
Collins, 2007.

Amazing insight and research into the power of creativity and the new creative economy. If you are in any doubt over the role of creativity in the world, then you need to read this book.

Thought Leaders — Matt Church, Scott Stein and
Michael Henderson

Thought Leaders is a growing community, of which I am part,
of clever people who are commercially smart. As the jacket says,
'this book helps capture, package and deliver for ideas for great
commercial success.

100 Great Icons — Chris Sheedy and Jenny Bond.
Random House Australia, 2006.

A great book filled with 100 ideas that made it big. I love stories
of creative endeavours that made good: this is full of them.

Linchpin — Are you indispensable? — Seth Godin.
Piatkus, 2010.

A great read on Seth Godin's unique view on why people who
break the boundaries and step out from the herd become
indispensable.

Clever — Rob Goffee and Gareth Jones.
Harvard Business Press, 2009.

A great book on the insights of leading smart and creative
people. Terrific research and great points of view.

How to Think Like a Futurist: Know First, Be First, Profit First —
Craig Rispin.
The Future Trends Group, 2009.

A terrific read on how to tap into future trends and think
ahead of the game. Craig's clarity is riveting and very useful in
understanding change and where the world is heading.

Disney's World — Leonard Mosley.
Scarborough House, 1990.

Being a big Disney fan, I loved this when I first read it. It's an
in-depth look at the life of one of my creative mentors and a
man who changed the world creatively.

Creating Zoos

How to Build a Business Culture that
Stimulates Creativity and Drives Innovation

WELCOME

Nigel Collin

International Authority in Leading Creatives

Creating Zoos

HOW TO BUILD A BUSINESS CULTURE THAT
STIMULATES CREATIVITY AND DRIVES INNOVATION

In the new creative economy, a company's IP is often
worth far more than their physical assets — just think
of Apple or Google.

If you don't foster a culture of creativity in your organisation,
you'll lose market share to those that do.

How do you build an business culture that supports and
stimulates your people's creative talents? You need a creative
zoo: a place where your creative people are happy and
productive, so you can use their talents and genius to the full.
A place that attracts and retains the best people, where coming
up with sexy, innovative ideas is simply part of what you do.

**This book shows you how to turn your company into a creativity
powerhouse that churns out million-dollar ideas thick and fast.**

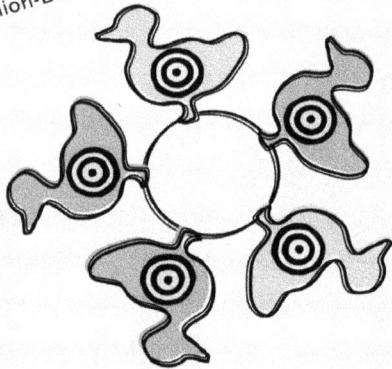

Shooting Ducks

Discover the 3 Essential Stages for Creating
Million-Dollar Ideas in Your Company

Nigel Collin

International Authority in Leading Creatives

Shooting Ducks

DISCOVER THE 3 ESSENTIAL STAGES FOR CREATING
MILLION-DOLLAR IDEAS IN YOUR COMPANY

Creatively, coming up with ideas is not the problem.

The world is full of ideas. Like ducks at a carnival sideshow, they just keep on coming. The trick is to hit them — and more importantly, to know which ones to hit for the really big prize.

You need the right creative process, one that can turn the creative controls on and off, and pick the winning ideas. That's how you become a market leader, hitting the jackpot time after time.

46% of business leaders we surveyed said they didn't have a process to harness and direct creativity.

This book offers you that process.

With Thanks

I don't want to have 17 pages of acknowledgements that no-one will ever read. But I do want to personally thank a number of people.

Firstly, all of you who contributed to the books with comments, quotes, case-studies, and the like. Most of you (I think all of you) are mentioned in the text, but I just want you to know that your input was invaluable and greatly appreciated.

Special thanks goes to Megan Kerr who edited the book and went way beyond the call of duty. Plus it was a pleasure to collaborate and throw ideas about. To Sha-mayne Chan of 2birds Design, for making the book visually stunning and for all her support. To Dale Beaumont for guiding the process. To Angelique Milojevic of Business Masterminds for her support and encouragement. And a big thanks to Matt Church for his direction and mentoring insights, as well as those of Craig Rispin.

Lastly, to my family, who have tolerated me tapping away at my computer and spreading documents everywhere, at home, in the car, and on holidays.

If I did forget anyone, please forgive me.

Where to from here:

Nigel offers a range of products and services to help business enterprise creativity and profit from it

___

NIGELCOLLIN.COM

Nigel's website offers a range of resources, videos' and blog to help businesses enterprise the creative talents of their people

___

CONFERENCE SPEAKING AND WORKSHOPS

Nigel is a dynamic and informative speaker and facilitator. He offers a range of keynote topics as well as in house workshops and master classes.

___

THE CREATIVE CATALYST PROGRAM

The Creative Catalyst is a business tool, combining an online diagnostic with business coaching, to help enterprise the creativity of your business.

support@nigelcollin.com
www.nigelcollin.com

Join the Quest

Subscribe to Nigel's blog, or visit the website, where you will find loads of resources and information to help better lead and inspire the creativity of others and help change the creative landscape of Australia

www.nigelcollin.com/blog

Nigel Collin is a champion of creativity.
He works with business leaders, helping
them commercialize the creative talents
of their people to get results and profit
from innovation.

For 9 years Nigel owned and ran Absurd Entertainment, an
entertainment design company, before passing on the baton
in 2004. He worked on a multitude of corporate and public
events including the 2000 Sydney Olympics and Paralympics
and The Sydney Royal Easter Show 1997-2003. He was Show
Director for Australia's largest-ever corporate event, in Sydney
in 2005.

Many companies across a myriad of industries including
IT, Entertainment, Design, Events, Marketing, Finance,
Pharmaceuticals, Government and Telecommunications have
benefited from Nigel's experience and expertise.

As a conference speaker and author, his work has Nigel has
worked around the globe. He is one of those rare people
whose passion for creativity and in-depth knowledge will
engage and inspire your people – and make a real difference
to your business.

Nigel's quest is to change the
creative landscape of the Australia.

To find out more visit **www.nigelcollin.com**

www.ingramcontent.com/pod-product-compliance
Lightning Source LLC
Chambersburg PA
CBHW070405200326
41518CB00011B/2070